The BATTLE PLAN for PRAYER

TEEN BIBLE STUDY

STEPHEN KENDRICK
ALEX KENDRICK

LifeWay Press®
Nashville, Tennessee

ISBN: 9781430039815

Dewey Decimal Classification: 248.84

Subject Heading: PRAYER/SPIRITUAL WARFARE/SPIRITUAL LIFE

Printed in the United States of America.

CONTENTS

ABOUT THE AUTHORS

Stephen Kendrick is a speaker, film producer, and author with a ministry passion for prayer and discipleship. He is a cowriter and producer of the movies *WAR ROOM, Courageous, Facing the Giants*, and *Fireproof* and cowriter of the New York Times bestsellers *The Resolution for Men* and *The Love Dare*. Stephen is an ordained minister and speaks at conferences and men's events. He attended seminary, received a communications degree from Kennesaw State University, and now serves on the board of the Fatherhood CoMission. Stephen and his wife, Jill, live in Albany, Georgia, with their six children, where they are active members of Sherwood Church.

Alex Kendrick is an award-winning author gifted at telling stories of hope and redemption. He is best known as an actor, writer, and director of the films *Fireproof, Courageous, Facing the Giants*, and *WAR ROOM* and coauthor of the New York Times bestselling books *The Love Dare, The Resolution for Men, Fireproof* (the novel), and *Courageous* (the novel). In 2002, Alex helped found Sherwood Pictures and partnered with his brother Stephen to launch Kendrick Brothers Productions. He is a graduate of Kennesaw State University and attended seminary before being ordained into ministry. Alex and his wife, Christina, live in Albany, Georgia, with their six children. They are active members of Sherwood Church.

INTRODUCTION

Knowing the dynamics of battle is key to success for any army. Those in command gather intelligence about the enemy, they create a plan of attack, and they prepare to respond appropriately to ensure victory. Wise leaders choose their battles and fight to win.

As believers it is time for us to get our battle plan ready. It is time for us to strategically prepare and fight for our homes and families. It is time for us, as the church, to stand up for truth. And prayer is a powerful weapon that is absolutely necessary to ensure our victory in this spiritual battle. So, welcome to *The Battle Plan for Prayer* Bible study.

We believe in the power of prayer. We've seen it in God's Word. We've seen prayer work in the lives of others. And we've experienced it firsthand in our own lives. We grew up in a praying home. Our church is a praying church. We have praying friends. It's undeniable to us that God willingly, readily, and powerfully answers prayer. Stories in the Bible may seem far-fetched until you experience God and answered prayer for yourself.

Many in our generation have lost sight of the power of prayer. We don't pray. Prayer is hard work. It's easier to go out and attempt to fix things ourselves than to pray. Because prayer requires us to be still, quiet, humble, dependent, and honest before a sovereign and holy God, prayer becomes our last resort. But prayer is so misunderstood and underutilized. What would happen if churches really began to pray again? What if believers got right with the Lord and began to seek His face again? Second Chronicles 7:14 reminds us that if "…My people who are called by My name humble themselves, pray and seek My face, and turn from their evil ways, then I will hear from heaven, forgive their sin, and heal their land." We believe God is raising up an army of prayer warriors in our generation. We are asking you to go with us on this journey and equip yourself and others to pray more effectively. We will discuss types of prayer, hindrances to prayer, keys to effective prayer, praying strategically for the lost and for believers alike. We will be sharing real stories of answered prayer in our lives and in Christian history, and we will be hearing from some of our generation's most respected prayer teachers and trainers and learning from them as well.

HOW TO USE

A WORD TO LEADERS...

The Battle Plan for Prayer is an eight-session study to help your students understand the importance of prayer and equip them to have a vibrant and effective prayer life.

The study consists of two main elements: 1) Group Session, and 2) Personal Devotions.

GROUP SESSION

Each group session begins with an introductory paragraph, then contains these elements:

» OPENING WORD

Use these opening illustrations and activities to introduce the session's message. They will help to make the session more memorable for students of various learning styles, break the ice, and build relationships within the group.

» Beginning with Session 2, you will also be prompted to review the previous session. This will give an opportunity to hear students share what they learned and experienced during their devotional times with the Lord.

» STUDY THE SCRIPTURE

Lead students to read the passages presented, then discuss the questions listed below each passage. Prior to the session, you will need to diligently study each Scripture passage and work through the questions so that you are equipped to lead the discussion. Prioritize Scripture study as you manage your group time.

» WHAT DO I DO NOW?

This is where the Scripture content is put into action. Lead your group to work through the application questions and activities.

» WHAT CAN I EXPECT?

This section will give your group a glimpse at what they can expect from the content of the five devotions that follow the group session.

PERSONAL DEVOTIONS

The personal devotions will reinforce what you have studied together in the group sessions. Encourage students to work though the devotions between group sessions and to use social media or other means to share what they are learning and how God is answering their prayers.

The last page of the personal devotions section is a journal page where students will be prompted to list truths that have impacted them through the week.

1

SESSION 1

DEVOTED
TO PRAYER

BATTLE PLAN |GROUP SESSION 1

DEVOTED TO PRAYER

Prayer is communicating with God within a loving relationship. It enables people to better know, love, and worship God personally. Prayer helps us to understand and conform our lives to God's perfect will and His ways. It aslo helps us access His power and resources, advance His spiritual rule and kingdom, and give Him the glory and honor He deserves. Prayer is transformation and makes us more like Jesus. Prayer is also powerful and can accomplish what a willing God can accomplish.

OPENING WORD

Take a moment to introduce yourself to everyone in your group. Discuss why you are going through this study and what you each hope to get out of it. How do you think this study will affect your relationship with God? As you begin, take turns sharing the most powerful answers to prayer you have experienced in your lives.

Realize that you are about to embark on something pretty cool together and that your relationship with one another and with God will definitely be blessed and changed. Understand that beginning a real relationship with God through Jesus is absolutely vital to enjoying an effective prayer life. To illustrate this, ask a few members of your group the following questions:

* If you had $1 million, would you let me have $1,000?
* Would you ever let me borrow your deodorant?
* Would you trust me with complete access to all of your emails, texts, and social media profiles for 2 days?

Why are those questions so awkward to ask each other? Only in a close, very trusted relationships would you feel the freedom to ask such questions. And you would probably only say "yes" to someone if the two of you were super close. and maintained a safe, committed friendship.

What does that reveal about the freedom or awkwardness we might experience when we pray?

STUDY THE SCRIPTURE: READ MARK 11:12-26

DISCUSS:

* What was something about prayer in this passage that jumped out at you?
* What did Jesus say God's house was supposed to be in verse 17 (quoting Isaiah 56:7)?
* In what way was the withered fig tree just like the fruitlessness and corruption in the temple?
* What does verse 24 teach us about prayer and faith?
* What do verses 25 and 26 teach us is necessary for an effective prayer life?

STUDY THE SCRIPTURE: READ JOHN 14:6,12-14

DISCUSS:

* What do these verses teach us about God that should encourage us to pray to Him this way? Is our God a personal God, or is He cold and distant?
* If someone has no relationship with Jesus, how can they approach God properly or with a clean heart? What should be the first prayer they pray? Do you have a genuine relationship with God through Jesus? If not, what holds you back from turning from your sins and to God right now and confessing Jesus as the Lord of your life? (Rom. 10:9)

WHAT DO I DO NOW?

Envision together what would happen if your entire student group became devoted to prayer. Share ideas about what your church would look like if it were to be a house of prayer for all nations. Take turns finishing the following sentences in a group discussion.

* "If I were more of a passionate prayer warrior, I would do more...."
* "If I were more of a passionate prayer warrior, I would do less..."
* "For our church to be a devoted house of prayer for all nations, I must..."
* "For our church to be a devoted house of prayer for all nations, we must...."

Now, pray as a group for all nations according to Mark 11:17.

WHAT CAN I EXPECT?

During your personal devotions, you will examine Scripture teachings from the New Testament that teach us more about prayer. You will begin to act upon these Scripture passages in a strategic way that will take your prayer life to the next level. Now, go to battle!

day 1

PRAYER 101

What is your reaction when you hear the word *prayer*? Do you feel comforted and at peace, or do you get nervous and feel guilty? Write some of your feelings about prayer in the space below as we jump into this study together.

When we stop to think about prayer, we quickly realize what a privilege it is. God does not have to communicate with us and doesn't need for us to communicate with Him. But, He chooses to. That's the love of God—He chooses to involve us in His work. He wants to have a relationship with us. He wants to show Himself mighty in our lives and intercede on our behalf time and time again.

When you really stop to think about it, what amazes you about prayer?

The heart of prayer is simply talking with God. In this study, we are going to get a better grasp on this vital practice and then take it a step further to create a strategy for prayer. You will learn to strategically pray for your family, classmates, and your lost friends. But, we have to start with the basics and lay a foundation before we can build up to large prayer strategies.

How would you define *prayer*? (Feel free to look up some definitions.)

Some of the words that came up in your definition might have included: ***petition, request, thanksgiving, praise.*** Consider sharing this definition with your group next time and hear what other people wrote as well.

If God compiled a list of the top five prayers He hears, what do you think would make the list?

Most likely, the list you compiled revolved around individual crises or routine rituals. Those prayers are important, but God's Word instructs believers to be devoted to prayer. This means we must move beyond the status quo. As we're beginning this study, maybe you're hesitant to add one more thing to your already busy schedule.

What is your greatest struggle with prayer? Finding time? Knowing what to pray?

Prayer isn't one more thing to add to your list. Prayer empowers the list. We are not asking you to add something new, but to do what you are already doing by relying on God's power and provision instead. We are challenging you to devote yourself to prayer.

One of the game changers when it comes to prayer is recognizing how much God loves us and wants to hear from us. When we stop to remember how much God longs for us to walk closely with Him, it really does change everything.

Take a moment to read Ephesians 3:16-18.

> *16 I pray that He may grant you, according to the riches of His glory, to be strengthened with power in the inner man through His Spirit, 17 and that the Messiah may dwell in your hearts through faith. I pray that you, being rooted and firmly established in love, 18 may be able to comprehend with all the saints what is the length and width, height and depth of God's love,*

Underline the words *pray* and *love* each time you see them.

How would your prayer life change if you prayed knowing that you were "rooted and firmly established in love"?

Prayer doesn't have to be something you are scared of or anxious about. If you remind yourself of your sure footing in the love of Christ, your prayers will hopefully come a little easier and be a little bolder. May God deepen your grasp of His love as you learn to boldly approach Him in a renewed devotion to prayer.

day 2

INSTRUCTIONS
ON PRAYER

Right above 1 Timothy 2 in the HCSB, the heading "INSTRUCTIONS ON PRAYER" is written. So, let's read verses 1-4 and unpack these instructions today:

> *¹ First of all, then, I urge that petitions, prayers, intercessions, and thanksgivings be made for everyone, ² for kings and all those who are in authority, so that we may lead a tranquil and quiet life in all godliness and dignity. ³ This is good, and it pleases God our Savior, ⁴ who wants everyone to be saved and to come to the knowledge of the truth.*

What other words are listed in verse 1 that mean *prayer***?**

For whom specifically does Paul say we should pray?

Why does prayer please God?

Our God is a good God who longs for His people to come to salvation. We will talk more later in the study about praying specifically for those who are lost, but for now let's think a little bigger.

You came to this study with a hope to be better equipped for prayer. Maybe you have a desire to pray more often, or to even begin to pray, or perhaps to pray with more intensity and focus. It is our hope that God will move you to a whole new level of prayer through this study. Begin by following the instructions in 1 Timothy that tell us to pray for everyone. Take time right now to list specific people you want to be more strategic in praying for.

Write your list below, then beside each name write one request you have for that person.

*

*

*

*

*

*

*

*

*

*

Now, go back through your list and pray specifically for each person.

We would love for you to bookmark this page so you can come back to this list over the next few weeks. This will help you remember to keep praying for these people and to also see how God will work and move through your prayers.

day 3

DEVOTED TO PRAYER

Paul commanded believers to be devoted to prayer (Rom. 12:12; Col. 4:2). While that sounds like a noble concept, what does that really mean? What does that type of devotion look like?

The Greek word for **devotion** Paul used in these verses is ***proskartereo***. The word is used ten times in the New Testament, five of which refer to prayer. To help us understand this type of prayer devotion, let's look at how the verb is used each time.

In the verses below, the translation of *proskartereo* is in bold. Note how it is used. Under each verse, explain what it teaches us about being devoted to prayer.

*   Acts 1:14 - All these were **continually** united in prayer, along with the women, including Mary the mother of Jesus, and His brothers.

*   Acts 2:42 - And they **devoted** themselves to the apostles' teaching, to the fellowship, to the breaking of bread, and to the prayers.

*   Acts 6:4 - But we will **devote** ourselves to prayer and to the preaching ministry.

*   Romans 12:12 - Rejoice in hope; be patient in affliction; be **persistent** in prayer.

*   Colossians 4:2 - **Devote** yourselves to prayer; stay alert in it with thanksgiving.

Summarize what these verses are saying about being devoted to prayer.

What difficulties or triumphs in your life have caused you to become more devoted to prayer?

What would need to change in your life for you to be more devoted to prayer? If it meant positively transforming your life and empowering your spiritual impact on others, would you be willing to make those changes?

In addition to the verses that used *proskartereo* ("devoted") concerning prayer, there are five other usages of the word in the New Testament. Studying these verses can actually help us get a better handle on how to become devoted to prayer.

In the verses below, the usage of *proskartareo* is in bold. Beside each verse, make notes of how this helps you better understand being "devoted" to prayer.

* Mark 3:9 - Then He told His disciples to have a small boat **ready** for Him, so the crowd would not crush Him.

* Acts 8:13 - Then even Simon himself believed. And after he was baptized, he **went around constantly** with Philip and was astounded as he observed the signs and great miracles that were being performed.

* Acts 10:7 - When the angel who spoke to him had gone, he called two of his household slaves and a devout soldier, who was one of those who **attended** him.

* Romans 13:6 - And for this reason you pay taxes, since the authorities are God's public servants, **continually attending** to these tasks.

How does the use of *proskartareo* in these verses help you understand what it means to be devoted to prayer?

Devotion involves committing to something consistently and frequently. To be consistently devoted to prayer, we have to train ourselves in this practice. It does not come naturally. We must train ourselves to be in constant communion with God.

Stop now to pray and ask God for help to repurpose your life as one who is devoted to prayer.

day 4

THE EXAMPLE OF JESUS

When most people think of Jesus' prayer life, they default to the teaching we commonly refer to as the Lord's Prayer. While we will dive deep into this pivotal prayer template later in this study, Jesus' prayer ministry was not isolated to this famous teaching. In fact, His entire ministry was saturated in prayer.

Read the following passages that describe the prayer life of Jesus. Under each verse, write what you learn about Jesus' prayer life.

* [Early stages of ministry] - Very early in the morning, while it was still dark, He got up, went out, and made His way to a deserted place. And He was praying there. (Mark 1:35)

* [Before making the selection of the twelve disciples] - During those days He went out to the mountain to pray and spent all night in prayer to God. (Luke 6:12)

* [After feeding the 5000] - After dismissing the crowds, He went up on the mountain by Himself to pray. When evening came, He was there alone. (Matt. 14:23)

* [Before His crucifixion] - He went out and made His way as usual to the Mount of Olives, and the disciples followed Him. When He reached the place, He told them, "Pray that you may not enter into temptation." Then He withdrew from them about a stone's throw, knelt down, and began to pray. (Luke 22:39-41)

How would you describe Jesus' prayer life?

At what times of day did Jesus pray?

In what kinds of situations did Jesus set aside time to pray?

Not only did Jesus teach on the importance of prayer, He modeled this devotion to prayer Himself.

Have you ever wondered why Jesus needed to pray? If Jesus was God, why did He need to take time to pray?

Although Jesus was fully God while He was on earth, Scripture also teaches that as He grew He "kept increasing in wisdom and stature, and in favor with God and men" (Luke 2:52, NASB). Prayer was Jesus' connection to God the Father while He lived on earth. Prayer was His means of knowing and carrying out God's will. Prayer was a vital part of the relationship between God the Father and Christ His Son.

Think of the most important relationship in your life. How strong would that relationship be if the communication between you stopped today?

Based on Jesus' prayer life, what is the primary function that prayer should serve?

If Jesus, the Son of God, was constantly dependent upon the Father through prayer, how could we possibly not think it is necessary for us?

As you close today, pray and ask God to show you some changes you need to make to become more consistent and dependent upon Him in prayer. (Hint: Being a part of this study is a huge step in the right direction. God will be faithful as you work to become devoted to prayer.)

day 5
PRAYER STRATEGY TARGET

It is our hope and prayer that you dive deep into the topic of prayer though this Bible Study. God will be faithful as you focus on prayer over these next seven sessions. It is also our prayer, that you leave this study with a firm grasp on how to pray for yourself and those around you—your friends, family members, the lost, those in authority over you, and more—in a strategic way.

To do that, we have developed a sort of road map—in the form of a Prayer Strategy Target.

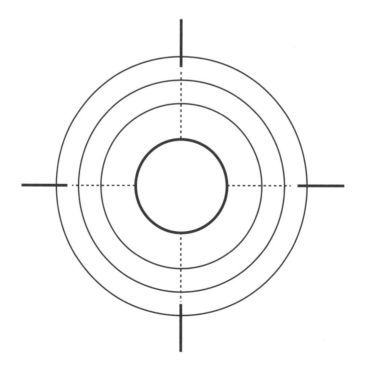

We will work through this target together over the coming weeks by focusing our Day 5 devotion on it. By the end of the study, you will know how to utilize this target and pray specifically and strategically for others.

We want to start today with the vertical and horizontal lines on the target. They represent the cross. Prayer begins with the cross of Jesus Christ.

Why is the cross so important?

Jesus' finished work on the cross has provided us access to the Father.

John 14:6 says: Jesus answered, "I am the way and the truth and the life. No one comes to the Father except through me" (NIV).

Our relationship to God through Jesus is the key to healthy and effective prayers. We need to be vertically aligned with God through the cross before we can do anything else.

As Scripture says, "He saved us, not on the basis of deeds which we have done in righteousness, but according to His mercy, by the washing of regeneration and renewing by the Holy Spirit, whom He poured out upon us richly through Jesus Christ our Savior, so that being justified by His grace we would be made heirs according to the hope of eternal life" (Titus 3:5-7, NASB).

If you are not a Christian, you will not see consistent success in your prayer life.

If you aren't certain of your relationship to God through Jesus, talk to your small group leader, your student pastor, or another godly adult about this decision. It is the most important one you'll ever make. They will be honored to help you.

> **If you've repented and trusted Jesus Christ as your Lord and Savior, this is the foundation for a strong prayer life. If you are clear in your heart that you have salvation, take time now to thank God for this incredible gift. Also, ask God to show you what areas of your life you're still trying to control instead of allowing Jesus to be Lord.**
> **Listen to what He says, then repent, writing your prayer of repentance.**

Now do something that might not seem so obvious. Pray about your prayer life. Write out a description of the kind of prayer warrior you desire to become. Then pray over that description, asking God to make that a reality in you.

May God do a great and lasting work in your heart and draw you deeper and closer into a loving relationship with Him like never before!

WEEKLY SUMMARY

List below three things you learned this week about prayer and how you'll apply these to your life.

    *

    *

    *

NOTES

Use the space below to jot down any other thoughts or questions you have about prayer in general or what you've studied this past week.

SCHEDULED AND SPONTANEOUS PRAYER

BATTLE PLAN |GROUP SESSION 2
SCHEDULED AND SPONTANEOUS PRAYER

In the last session, we introduced the subject of prayer and the idea of becoming devoted to prayer. In this session we will break down devotion to prayer into two practical methods: prayer that is SCHEDULED and prayer that is SPONTANEOUS. Whether we pray because we have set aside time to pray or because we have been prompted by something to pray, we must learn to soak our lives in on-going prayer. Teenagers "text without ceasing." God wants us to learn to "pray without ceasing."

Rejoice always! Pray constantly. Give thanks in everything, for this is God's will for you in Christ Jesus. **(1 THESS. 5:16-18)**

OPENING WORD

Take turns sharing with the group the amount of time you probably spent yesterday...

* _____ Watching TV
* _____ Watching movies
* _____ Watching movies you have already seen
* _____ Texting somemone
* _____ Texting or messaging someone who was in the same room
* _____ Praying

Replace with: When we say that we don't really have time to pray, what we're saying is that we don't MAKE time to pray. Everyone on the planet has the same number of minutes in every day. We all will reveal our priorities daily by what we choose to do with those minutes.

STUDY THE SCRIPTURE: READ ACTS 2:37-42

DISCUSS:

* Peter had just preached an amazing sermon. What was the result according to verse 41?
* What were the main things these new believers devoted themselves to according to verse 42?
* What does it mean that they ***devoted*** themselves to prayer? Think back to last week's devotions.
* This newborn insta-mega church had just seen thousands of people saved. They then devoted themselves to prayer and experienced God's power in amazing ways. What would happen if your church and others in your community devoted yourselves to prayer? How do you think it would impact your church body, your families, and your influence in the community?

Prompts for spontaneous prayer:
Anything can remind us to pray! There are many situations, needs, and events that take place in our lives that should prompt us to pray. Check out the list below. Take turns and have different students read the Scripture that points us to prayer in each case. Discuss each instance and list others. Share ways in which God has answered some of these types of prayers for you in the past:

* Boldness - Praying for courage to share the gospel. **Read Ephesians 6:18-19.**
* Needs - Ask God for what you need each day. **Read Matthew 6:11**
* Confusion and Crisis - Confidently ask God for wisdom. **Read James 1:5-8.**
* Sin - Confess sin to God right away. **Read 1 John 1:9** and **Matthew 6:12-13.**
* Stress - Give your worries to God. **Read 1 Peter 5:6-7.**
* Rejoicing - Pray when things are great. **Read 1 Thessalonians 5:16-18.**

If you pray at a scheduled time for a few minutes each day and also let different things prompt you to pray spontaneously throughout your day, you can be almost "praying without ceasing" before you know it!

WHAT DO I DO NOW?

Schedule a time to pray each day. Make note of a specific time and place you will pray tomorrow. If your mobile device has a calendar on it, give yourself a reminder right now and show that reminder to the group for accountability. Journal that time and place below:

My prayer time: _____ My prayer place:_____

Close by praying together as a group that God will help you to not only make prayer a daily habit in your schedule, but also prompt you to quietly pray as things happen during your day. Be prepared to share next session how God called you to pray and what happened as a result.

WHAT CAN I EXPECT?

This coming week's devotions will dig deeper into planned prayer and spontaneous prayer. Also, we will see what the horizontal line in the Prayer Strategy Target is all about.

day 1

SCHEDULED PRAYER, PART 1

In a study like this one, it's easy to get excited about prayer without actually accomplishing it. Instead of merely getting energized about a battle plan for prayer, you need to ensure that you set yourself up to follow through.

As we continue this journey, take some practical steps to ensure you will be persistent in prayer. As we talked about in our group session, some prayer times are scheduled and some are spontaneous. We will look at scheduled prayer today and tomorrow and spontaneous prayer later this week.

> **Read Jesus' description of how He said we should pray in Matthew 6:5-8. Underline or circle key words and phrases.**
>
> *⁵ Whenever you pray, you must not be like the hypocrites, because they love to pray standing in the synagogues and on the street corners to be seen by people. I assure you: They've got their reward! ⁶ But when you pray, go into your private room, shut your door, and pray to your Father who is in secret. And your Father who sees in secret will reward you. ⁷ When you pray, don't babble like the idolaters, since they imagine they'll be heard for their many words. ⁸ Don't be like them, because your Father knows the things you need before you ask Him.*

> **What are three things you discovered about prayer from this passage?**
>
> *
>
> *
>
> *

What is Jesus condemning in these verses?

Jesus is not condemning the act of public prayer itself, but rather the wrong motive.

Who is the intended audience for our prayers?

Prayer is ultimately not about you, but about God. It is not about your glory or will, but about His glory and His will. Jesus encourages true believers to take prayer into a private place because our prayers are not for impressing others, but for knowing and pleasing God alone.

In our group session, you designated a time a place to pray today. Did you hold to that commitment? Why or why not?

Do you have a private room designated for prayer on a regular basis—a prayer closet or a special spot? Do you have a specific time you meet with God? Why or why not?

You may not have the physical space in your home to claim a separate room as a private prayer sanctuary, but you can make some adjustments to set yourself up for success when it comes to prayer. Designate a spot in your room, or speak with your parents about setting aside a place that is just for prayer.

How can you reclaim a space and a time in your home to pray regularly?

Hold yourself accountable. In the space below, write down a place and time that you will set aside for prayer for the remainder of this week.

day 2

SCHEDULED PRAYER, PART 2

Let's look at some examples from the Bible of people setting aside specific times and places just for the purpose of prayer.

David chose specific times to pray. Read Psalm 55:16-17 below.

> *¹⁶ As for me, I call to God,*
> *and the LORD saves me.*
> *¹⁷ Evening, morning and noon*
> *I cry out in distress,*
> *and he hears my voice.* (NIV)

When did David pray according to this passage?

David's example is inspiring. It's a honor that we can look back thousands of years and read so many of his specific prayers in the Psalms. Not all of David's prayers were joyful prayers. In the verses shown, he is crying out in distress to God, but notice he does it in a strategic, scheduled way.

Later in the Psalms, David talks again about scheduled prayer. Read Psalm 119:164.

How many times did David say he prays?

Daniel was another who scheduled time to pray on a consistent basis. Read Daniel 6:10-11.

> *¹⁰ When Daniel learned that the document had been signed, he went into his house. The windows in its upper room opened toward Jerusalem, and three times a day he got down on his knees, prayed, and gave thanks to his God, just as he had done before.*
> *¹¹ Then these men went as a group and found Daniel petitioning and imploring his God.*

What you can't tell just by reading these verses is that Daniel was in a time of extreme trouble during this season of his life. He knew that he would be potentially arrested and killed for his faith. Even then, Daniel prayed and trusted. God answered his prayers and rescued him from the mouths of lions.

How many times on average would you estimate that you pray each day?

How many of those times are scheduled and how many are spontaneous?

You may not be able to start to have seven times of scheduled prayer a day, or even three. But, we challenge you to at least start with one time. If you desire to add more, then great, but at least start with one scheduled time and see if you can keep it up throughout the course of this study. We are confident that as you devote scheduled time to prayer, you are going to see it impact your life.

Write down a specific time you plan to pray this week. Jot a reminder on a sticky note or set an alarm on your phone as a way to remember the time you've committed to scheduled prayer.

We will talk more about spontaneous prayers over the next few days, as both spontaneous and scheduled prayers are important in a believer's life.

day 3

SPONTANEOUS PRAYER, PART 1

It is extremely helpful to have a scheduled time and a sacred space in which you pray. Scripture also teaches us to pray continually. Unexpected obstacles and situations will arise throughout your week. During those moments you will find yourself needing to pray. Be prepared for those spontaneous times.

Read 1 Thessalonians 5:17 and write it in the space below.

Depending on your translation of Scripture, the word used in this verse might be *constantly*, *regularly*, *continually*, or *without ceasing*. On a corporate level, churches can "pray without ceasing" by taking turns and praying in shifts throughout the day. On an individual level, we can make prayer a natural and regular part of our day.

Do you believe that this instruction is actually possible? Why or why not?

What would it look like for this verse to be practically applied in your life this week?

As you think through your schedule over the next 24 hours, there are probably some times where you are going to need to go to God in prayer and your prayer closet will not be accessible.

In the next 24 hours, when would be pivotal times during the day you could pause and pray?

Identifying pivotal times to pray is important and one of the first steps in becoming more devoted to
prayer. But we can't always predict when we will need to take time to pray. In order to truly put 1 Thessalonians 5:17 into practice, we must remain in close fellowship with God and be aware of His presence in our lives. The ultimate goal is for prayer to be a regular and frequent habit throughout your day.

Come up with an action plan. Your plan may include hanging notes in strategic places, setting reminders on your phone, or asking your parents to hold you accountable. In the space below, write at least three tangible reminders you can use to increase your prayer frequency over the next 24 hours. Once your plan is in place, commit it to God through prayer.

We will finish this devotion discussing different times for spontaneous prayers. The more you get in the habit of bringing conversation with God into a daily rhythm in your life, the more you can sense and feel God's presence and guidance day in and day out.

BOLDNESS

If you are a follower of Christ, there will be multiple opportunities for you to share your faith or stand for the truth. All of those moments call for spontaneous prayer.

What moments in the recent past have you had the opportunity to share the gospel with someone or take a stand for truth? Did you have the courage and boldness to follow through?

Spend some time right now praying that God would give you courage to be bold for Him in every situation. List two new situations and pray for them.

NEEDS

Each day we will have different needs arise in our lives. God knows what these needs are and longs to meet them.

What are the needs in your life? List two needs below and spend a moment praying about them.

day 4

SPONTANEOUS PRAYER, PART 2

Today we will finish our discussion about specific reminders for spontaneous prayers. Remember, when conversation with God becomes a part of your daily rhythm, you will be able to sense His presence and guidance even more. Let's finish looking at occasions that should prompt us toward spontaneous prayer.

CONFUSION

Isaiah 55:9 says that God's thoughts are higher than our thoughts. We often can't see the big picture, so it is understandable to have times of confusion.

What is something that is confusing in your life right now? Ask God to help you see more clearly. Write your prayer and pray it to Him.

CRISIS

It's likely that you or someone you know is in a crisis situation. Just take a look at one of your social media feeds. When you see someone in crisis, stop and pray for them.

Write any situation God brings to mind in this category for yourself or someone else. Take a moment to lift this concern to God.

SIN

Nothing blocks your prayer life like unconfessed sin. If you have sin in your life, you need to repent in order to re-establish healthy communion with the Father. Don't cover it up, dismiss it, and try to forget about it. Repent and confess.

List specific sins you'd need to confess. Repent and ask God to forgive you.

STRESS

Every person faces stress. Probably even right now something is tugging on your mind, maybe something that you have to do, or perhaps a relationship that is challenging. Get in the habit of bringing those stresses to our Father.

List the top three things you are stressed about at this time and lay those before God.

BLESSINGS

Spontaneous prayer shouldn't just happen when times are difficult. We should break out in prayer when God blesses us. He is good and longs to give good gifts to His children. (See Matt. 7:11.)

List some of the blessings you have received from God. Take a moment to thank Him for being so good.

BURDENS

Read Matthew 11:28. God wants us to bring Him our burdens.

List some of the burdens you are carrying. Bring those to the Lord right now.

REQUESTS

God wants us to bring our requests to Him, but He also wants us to bring them with the right motives. (See James 4:3.) Check your motives when you bring your requests.

List below some requests you want to present to God. Make sure your motivation is pure as you bring those requests to Him.

REJOICING

Philippians 4:4 says, "Rejoice in the Lord always." We have so much to rejoice over, even in hard times.

Spend a moment writing reasons you have to rejoice. Speak those to God in praise and thanksgiving.

day 5

PRAYER STRATEGY
TARGET

As promised, in each Day 5 we are going to spend time working through our Prayer Strategy Target. Here is a reminder of what it looks like:

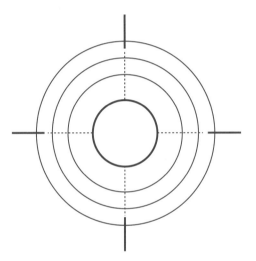

Last week we evaluated our vertical relationship with God and were reminded of how prayer is made possible through Jesus' death on the cross.

This week we want to look at the horizontal line across the middle of the target. It represents being aligned well with others in order for prayer to be most effective. God wants us to walk in love and in unity with those around us. Bitterness toward others can hinder our prayer lives. Also, if we have wronged someone and not made it right, God wants us to stop delaying and to set things right.

We will focus on this topic in more depth throughout the study, but let's pause and evaluate where we are on that horizontal line just for a moment together.

An interesting passage in Genesis 11 describes the construction of the tower of Babel. In this biblical account, ungodly people decided to build a city with an enormous tower for their own glory and prestige. They planned it out and began the challenge, and at first found success in their efforts. But God looked down from heaven and basically said, "Because of their unity, nothing will be impossible for them." (See v. 6.) So He intervened. He divided them by changing their communication into numerous languages to prevent them from finishing their prideful monument. In the confusion and chaos, they abandoned the project and separated themselves by language, spreading out across the land.

What is so striking about this passage of Scripture is that God Himself noted that when people are unified, they are able to exert tremendous power and momentum. Even ungodly people! So imagine how powerful unity can be for people who worship and obey the God of the universe. If they seek the Lord and act in unity, nothing can stop them.

That's why the Enemy does everything possible to keep God's people divided. Because once we come together in unity, we gain momentum and take ground for the kingdom. United prayer is powerful. But prayer from a divided people … well, not so much. This is why removing bitterness toward others and choosing to forgive is so crucial. In fact, any pride or selfishness should be seen as an enemy of unified prayer.

In John 17, Jesus prayed a beautiful prayer, asking God to unify believers into one body, that the world would know He was sent by God to bring salvation to the world (v. 21). Psalm 133:1 echoes the same theme: "Behold, how good and how pleasant it is for brothers to dwell together in
unity! (NASB)

Read John 13:34-35.

Jesus' words here are clear, and the model Jesus gave us through His life and ministry makes it even more clear—we are to love our neighbor. And our neighbor is everyone.

So, before we can tackle this concept of prayer in a serious way, we need to not only evaluate our relationship with God, but also our relationship with others.

Take a moment and consider any strained or broken relationships that you have in your life. Talk with God about these relationships and ask Him what you need to do in order to make these right again.

Relationships are complicated, we know, but the Bible says:

If it is possible, as far as it depends on you, live at peace with everyone.
ROMANS 12:18 (NIV)

WEEKLY SUMMARY

List below three things you learned this week about prayer and how you'll apply these to your life.

*

*

*

NOTES

Use the space below to jot down any other thoughts or questions you have about prayer in general or what you've studied this past week.

TYPES OF PRAYERS

BATTLE PLAN | GROUP SESSION 3

TYPES OF PRAYERS

Prayer has many forms and types that can fit almost any situation. What are basic types of prayers and how does God answer them? Not every prayer is a request. Some prayers are statements. Not every word of worship is sung to music. Some are spoken to God in prayer. In this study, we will discuss the acronym A.C.T.S. which stands for Adoration, Confession, Thanksgiving, and Supplication.

OPENING WORD

Use the table below and discuss these analogies to prayer. Let one member of the group say the statement in the left column, then everyone shout out other ideas to add to the right column.

Prayer is like a water fountain because it...	...refreshes the weary and the thirsty.
Prayer is like a nuclear warhead because it...	...can move mountains.
Prayer is like Armageddon because it...	...is part of a battle; a battle that God wins!
Prayer is like high-speed internet because it...	...connects you with God right away.
Prayer is like a radio antenna because it...	...allows you to tune in to God's will.
Prayer is like a psycologist's couch because...	...it lets you share your secrets with God.
Prayer is like a cell phone, but without the...	...dead zones, batteries, bills, and contracts.

STUDY THE SCRIPTURE: TYPES OF PRAYERS

ADORATION: Prayer that praises and worships God. Read Matthew 6:9-10 and 1 Chronicles 29:10-13

* How does Jesus open the model prayer with adoration? Why is that important?
* How does beginning our prayer with adoration affect the rest of our prayer?
* What's the setting for David's prayer in 1 Chronicles 29:10-13? What kind of prayer did David pray? In what verse do you see him praise God for who He is? In what verse does he recount what God has done?

CONFESSION: Being honest with God and repenting of our sins. Read Psalm 51:1-13

* David prayed this prayer of confession after his sin with Bathsheba. What kind of prayer was this?
* Does David ever pass the blame for his sin? Does he polish his sin to make it look less sinful? Does he ever make excuses for his sin? Explain.
* What does this teach us about prayers of confession?

THANKSGIVING: God-directed, humbly-expressed gratitude. Read Hebrews 13:15; Ephesians 5:3-4; and Colossians 3:15-17

What does it mean to *continually* thank God as stated in Hebrews 13:15?
* Instead of all the sinful things listed in Ephesians 5:3-4, what are Christians supposed to exhibit?
* What is the basic theme of Colossians 3:15-17?

SUPPLICATION: Asking for something from God. It means to beseech, petition, or appeal for God to do or provide something for yourself or others. (Eph. 6:18) The Bible says, "You do not have because you do not ask" (James 4:2).
* What does it teach us about God's nature that we are invited to ask, seek, and knock?
* Jesus taught us to pray to God our Father in Matthew 6:9-13. How does that theme return in Matthew 7:7-11?

WHAT DO I DO NOW?

Spend time praying as a group, using these types of prayer. Begin with adoration, praising God for what He's done in your lives and church. Next spend time in confession and repentance of sins. Follow that with thanksgiving. Finish with supplication, asking God to meet various needs of yourselves and others. Be specific.

WHAT CAN I EXPECT?

In this week's devotions, we will put the Prayer Strategy Target to use as a part of our plan for battle against temptation. We will also dig into each of the aspects of the Lord's Prayer.

day 1
YOUR NAME BE HOLY

⁹Our Father in heaven, Your name be honored as holy. ¹⁰Your kingdom come, Your will be done on earth as it is in heaven.

MATTHEW 6:9-10

For this week's devotions, we are going to unpack the Lord's Prayer by focusing on the individual petitions that Jesus taught us to make. The first petition is a desire for the name of God to be honored as holy. His name should be set apart as greater and more special than all other names. His name—like His attributes—is like none other. Calling upon the name of the Lord is like dialing His specific phone number. It initiates direct communication with God Almighty.

Read Exodus 20:7. What are some ways people misuse the name of the Lord?

Why is this significant enough for God to address in one of the Ten Commandments?

Read Philippians 2:10-11. Scripture teaches that not everyone will follow Jesus and go to heaven (Matt. 25:31-46), so what do you think it means that every knee will bow at Jesus' name and every tongue confess that He is Lord?

Read Psalm 135:13. How is God's reputation related to His name?

We must remember that prayer is not based upon our name, but God's name. God's name alone is Holy, reigning, supreme. It is perfect, and more powerful than any name. More honored. Higher than every other name. It invites God's presence. It rebukes evil. It saves us. It is to be worshiped. That's why we must never take any of God's names in vain or use them flippantly. Rather, we praise and worship His name while honoring His attributes, power, and authority.

The next petition in the model prayer asks for God's Kingdom and will to advance on the earth. Again, prayer is not about our plans and kingdom, but His. When we pray, we are not seeking to bend God to our ever-changing, imperfect desires. We are yielding our lives to His perfect and eternal will. May His Kingdom come and His will be done.

> **What is God's will? Look up the verses below and write down beside each verse what God's will is, according to each passage.**
>
> **1 Timothy 2:3-4**
>
> **Micah 6:8**
>
> **1 Thessalonians 5:18**
>
> **1 Thessalonians 4:3**

As we pray, God amazingly reveals His will and ways to us, and then starts to align our hearts and minds with His. We yield to His perfect and powerful lordship. Christ is the "head of the body, the church," worthy of being ascribed "first place in everything" (Col. 1:18). As Jesus prayed, "not my will, but Yours be done.." we too should pray, "Your kingdom come and Your will be done ... in me and in my life." We follow where He lovingly leads.

> In your time of prayer today, focus on the name of God. Pray that His name would be trusted and always honored in your life. Also, submit to God by faith and and ask that His Kingdom to come and His will to be done in your life right now and in today's circumstances that you are going through. Then, expect great things to happen as a result.

day 2

OUR DAILY BREAD

Give us today our daily bread.
MATTHEW 6:11

This petition is asking God to provide for our needs. After their Exodus from Egypt, the nation of Israel wandered through the wilderness and complained of their lack of food and water. God promised to "rain bread from heaven" (Ex. 16:4) for the people. One interesting fact about this bread was its unique nature as a daily provision.

Then the Lord said to Moses, "I am going to rain bread from heaven for you. The people are to go out each day and gather enough for that day. This way I will test them to see whether or not they will follow My instructions.
EXODUS 16:4

Why did God want the people to gather just enough for that day rather than stockpiling the food?

¹¹ The Lord spoke to Moses, ¹² "I have heard the complaints of the Israelites. Tell them: At twilight you will eat meat, and in the morning you will eat bread until you are full. Then you will know that I am Yahweh your God."
EXODUS 16:11-12

How did God's provision correspond with the people's understanding of Him?

Just like He promised, God provided for the people. When the people saw the "fine flakes" of bread on the ground, "they asked one another, 'What is it?' because they didn't know what it was" (Ex. 16:14-15). The word *manna* literally means, *what is it*.

These former slaves had become dependent upon the provision of their taskmasters. Now free from their control and their provision, they were without access to basic needs. In this dependent and helpless state, God provided for them. It was a test to trust Him daily for what they needed. There was no planning for the future. They had to trust God one day at a time.

Think about ways in which you are dependent upon others such as your parents. Do you trust the person on whom you are dependent? Why or why not?

Hopefully, you see the connection between the Exodus narrative and Jesus' prayer. "Our Father, will you give us our daily bread?" We are not working about tomorrow's bread. We are asking for today's physical and spiritual needs and nourishment to be provided by God's provisional hand. We are focusing on the real needs at hand — one day at a time.

We acknowledge our utter dependence on Him: God, if you don't feed us, we won't eat.

What do you genuinely need right now? Have you prayed about it?

What are the genuine needs of your church right now? Have you prayed about them?

Instead of doing what you can do to fix these situations, ask God to show Himself again as the Lord who provides (Gen. 22:14).

Pray for God's provision today.

day 3

FORGIVE US OUR DEBTS

And forgive us our debts, as we also have forgiven our debtors.
MATTHEW 6:12

This petition is unique compared to the others. This request for pardon comes with a distinct requirement: forgive us as we have forgiven others.

We understand that we need forgiveness. None of us is righteous: all have sinned against God (Rom. 3:23). We know that the wages of sin is death (Rom. 6:23). Therefore, we are in need of judicial forgiveness from God—a once-for-all pardon that allows us to receive salvation. Once we have that type of forgiveness, we are justified before God, at peace with God, and have righteousness from God through faith in Christ. Our salvation is as secure as the eternally powerful hands that hold it. (John 10:27-29)

When Jesus died upon the cross, how many of your sins had not been committed yet?

Why, then, do you believe we ask God to forgive our sins regularly if He has already forgiven them once and for all?

We ask regularly for forgiveness because in addition to needing judicial forgiveness we also need relational forgiveness. For example, when you disobey your parents, that doesn't change your relationship (or position) with them. You will always be their son or daughter. Your disobedience doesn't change your position. However, it does change the fellowship of your relationship. If you have received the gospel and God has made you a new creation (2 Cor. 5:17), the status of your relationship with God does not change. You don't need to get saved and be justified again every time you sin. But you are in need of relational forgiveness and must walk in the light and in honest confession before God if you want to stay in close fellowship with Him (1 John 1:5-10).

The penitent heart you present before God acknowledges you have sinned and you are sorry about what you have done (Ps. 51:3-4). But a truly repentant heart will turn from the sin of "unforgiveness" and extend forgiveness to others as well.

With that frame of understanding, answer these questions:

Do I really want to pray that God would show me the kind of grace I have shown others? Explain.

What words would you use to describe the manner in which you have forgiven others?

Oftentimes, we may reword our "unforgiveness" like this:

* Well, I can forgive but I refuse to forget."

* "I forgive them but I never want to be around them."

* "I'll forgive them only after they suffer a while and get what's coming to them."

Read 2 Corinthians 5:17. What does this tell you about how God forgives.

Jesus' forgiveness is once and for all. When we are forgiven of our sins, we are a new creation. God does not dwell on our old selves—our sin—but looks at us through the righteousness of Christ. Is there anyone you need to forgive? Someone who wronged you but you keep holding anger in your heart against them?

Pray today that you may be able to extend a heart of forgiveness for that person. Ask God to help you to always willingly forgive others in the same manner He willingly forgives you.

day 4

DO NOT BRING US INTO TEMPTATION

And do not bring us into temptation, but deliver us from the evil one.

MATTHEW 6:13

These final two petitions pray for protection from temptation and the Evil One. It is a cry for help to keep us away from things that would damage our integrity.

Don't miss the power of the plural pronouns here. What Jesus prayed is important but what He didn't pray is also important. He didn't pray: "Do not bring ME into temptation, but deliver ME from the evil one." This kind of individualistic, independent mindset was not part of His prayer. If one person commits sin, the entire group deals with the consequences. Regardless of what we think, our decisions affect others greatly.

Stop for a minute and really think about the gravity of your decisions. If you fall into temptation, how would that impact your family?

If you fall into temptation, how would that impact your friends, teammates, and classmates?

If you are not walking closely with God, how would that impact your church?

My sin affects us. Your sin affects us. None of us is an island. We are the church, the body of Christ. When the foot suffers, the entire body staggers (1 Cor. 12:26).

Read Matthew 6:13 again. When Jesus prayed that God would not bring us into temptation, this statement does not mean that God normally employs such methods. We know that God is not tempted by evil and He Himself does not tempt anyone (Jas. 1:13). God has also promised that every time we are tempted He provides a way of escape (1 Cor. 10:13). Jesus is able to come to our aid since He was tempted just like us yet He never sinned.

Instead, our prayer should be more: "God, keep me on Your righteous path. Sound the alarm when temptation is near. Keep my eyes open and heart alert. Remind me that I could fall into the very sin that I hate. Cause me to hate and acknowledge any sin that so easily ensnares me. Awaken me to the reality of an enemy who prowls around like a roaring lion seeking to devour (1 Pet. 5:8)."

> **At this point, let's get specific. If you feel uncomfortable writing down details in this book—feel free to shorthand it or code it somehow—but answer this honestly:**
>
> **If the Evil One wanted to take me out, what strategy would he likely use? What temptation would he employ? In what areas have I been pridefully letting my guard down?**

By the way, if you don't have an answer for this question, you may be in a dangerous blind spot and closer to spiritual ruin than you think. Take this opportunity to pray more defensively so that you will not be taken advantage of by Satan's schemes (2 Cor. 2:11). Talk with God and make a battle plan on how you can keep from falling to the temptation you mentioned above. Be specific.

> **If these temptations come in certain environments which you can avoid, talk with God and make a battle plan. Get specific. What temptations do you need help avoiding? What strategies of the Enemy do you need to realize? Pray through these areas and ask God for deliverance from our evil adversary.**

day 5

PRAYER STRATEGY TARGET

Today we need to discuss one more foundational piece to the prayer target.

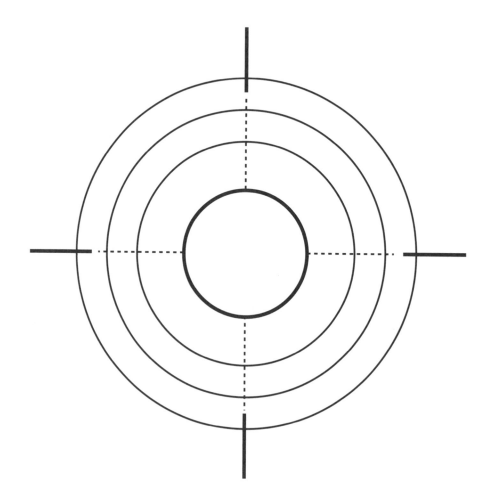

The circle in the middle will be where you eventually write the names of some persons you are praying for, but today we want to talk about that circle itself. On the chart you will see that the circle in the middle is a reddish color. That is because it represents the heart of the person praying. The condition of your heart affects your prayers.

Read James 5:16 and Psalm 66:18. Summarize these verses in the space below.

No one is saying you have to be perfect, but what these verses are saying is that the condition of your heart does matter when you pray.

James said the reason for a delay in God's answer is not always a timing issue. Sometimes "you ask and do not receive, because you ask with wrong motives, so that you may spend it on your pleasures" (Jas. 4:3). If lust, greed, bitterness, or pride is at the heart of a request, God may decline it in order to guard us from the hurt or idolatry that could result from the toxic request.

The first chapter of Proverbs says, "They will call on me, but I will not answer; They will seek me diligently but they will not find me, because they hated knowledge and did not choose the fear of the Lord" (vv. 28–29). Their attitude and behavior—the true condition of their hearts—stood between their request for help and its arrival. If they were ready to listen, however, if they would get their hearts right, their plight would be much better.

What is the condition of your heart right now? Are you hiding sin or harboring bitterness? How is the Lord convicting you? Pray, allowing God to reveal the true condition of your heart. As He reveals sin, repent so that your heart would be pure as you approach Him in prayer.

Read and pray Psalm 139:23-24. Spend some time making any notes and praying about the motives of your heart and get that right with God.

WEEKLY SUMMARY

List below three things you learned this week about prayer and how you'll apply these to your life.

    *

    *

    *

NOTES

Use the space below to jot down any other thoughts or questions you have about prayer in general or what you've studied this past week.

SESSION 4

LOCKS
AND KEYS
OF PRAYER

BATTLE PLAN | GROUP SESSION 4

LOCKS AND KEYS OF PRAYER

God designed, created, and maintains how prayer works. When praying, we must approach God on His terms, not ours. He tells us in His Word that our relationship with Him, how we are treating others, and the condition of our hearts will either help or hinder our prayers. We will call the hindrances to our prayers "locks" and the things that help our prayers, we will call "keys."

OPENING WORD

As a group, take a few minutes to share stories about times you received something special that you asked for from your parents or guardians. Discuss the condition of your relationship with your parents at the time of requesting and receiving. Were you being respectful and obedient or rebellious?

If your child were being repeatedly disobedient and disrespectful to you, would you give him or her anything he or she asked for? Explain.

How does this relate to your prayer relationship with God?

STUDY THE SCRIPTURE: PRAYER LOCKS

God's Word reveals to us that the following things will hurt or hinder our prayer lives.

* **Showing off: Read Matthew 6:5-6.**
  Why do people who pray just to show-off receive nothing from God?

* **Babbling: Read Matthew 6:7-8.**
  According to verse 8, why does repeating the same meaningless words hinder our prayers?

* **Not praying: Read James 4:1-2.**
  Go figure: prayers not prayed go unanswered. Is that God's fault, or ours? Why?

* **Being unsaved: Read John 14:6.**
  What is the only way any of us could possibly gain access to God the Father?

* **Not repenting: Read Psalm 66:18.**
  Why does God not answer the prayers of people who refuse to stop sinning?

* **Being greedy: Read James 4:3.**
  What should our motives be when we ask God for things?

* **Being cruel: Read 1 Peter 3:7.**
  Why would God not answer the prayers of someone who has mistreated others?

* **Being bitter: Read Mark 11:25-26.**
  Why would unforgiveness be a hinderance in our prayer life?

STUDY THE SCRIPTURE: THE KEYS TO PRAYER

God's Word reveals to us that the following things will hurt or hinder our prayer lives.

* **Being persistent (Not giving up on God): Read Luke 11:5-10.**
  Does this mean we have to pester God to get Him to answer? Explain.

* **Praying in secret: Read Matthew 6:5-6.**
  Why should we pray in our secret place?

* **Praying in agreement with others: Read Matthew 18:19-20.**
  In what ways is praying with others different from praying alone?

* **Repenting and getting right with God: Read James 5:16.**
  Are obedient children more likely to ask for things that their parents also want?

* **Fasting while praying: Read Acts 14:23.**
  What does it mean to fast?

* **Staying close to God and in His Word: Read John 15:7.**
  What kind of prayers does an avid Bible-reader pray?

* **Praying in Jesus' name: Read John 14:12-14.**
  What does it mean to pray in Jesus' name?

* **Praying in line with God's will: Read 1 John 5:14.**
  How can you pray according to God's will?

* **Praying in faith: Read Mark 11:24**
  Are you approaching God in faith by trusting in His power and goodness?

WHAT DO I DO NOW?

Now spend time praying for each other and asking God to help you completely get rid of anything that hinders your prayers and to pray according to the keys of prayer in a close and faith-filled relationship with God.

WHAT CAN I EXPECT?

During your devotions this week, you will turn these prayer keys into prayer habits and will finally put pen to paper on your Prayer Target.

day 1

LOCKS, PART 1

Today and tomorrow, we are going to look at some biblical passages that tell us why God might not be answering our prayers. They will serve as warnings to us, no matter what phase of life we are in.

LOCK 1: UNCONFESSED SIN

Read Isaiah 59:1-2 and fill out the chart below.

What Hinders Prayer	Why is This Important

Israel had questioned why the Lord had not heard their cries to Him (Isaiah 58:3). In the verses above, Isaiah assured the nation of Israel that the reason their prayers were not answered was not because God is not powerful enough or even because He does not hear. It was because of their unconfessed sin. The people were not only sinful, they were unrepentant, resulting in a barrier between them and God.

Is there anything you need to confess to the Lord today? Do that right now.

Read Psalm 66:18-19 and fill out the chart below accordingly.

What Hinders Prayer	Why is This Important

What does it mean to have malice in your heart?

Malice is the desire to see harm, suffering, or evil come upon someone else. You might attempt to soften your feelings of resentment towards someone by saying that you don't want evil to come upon them, but you simply don't want to see good come to them. In reality, if you don't desire someone to experience good in life, you are essentially desiring evil for him or her. The absence of good is evil.

When you become aware of malice in your heart, what is the appropriate response?

God may not be addressing your prayers because you are not addressing your sin. Ask God to make you aware of other sin in your heart and confess that to Him. Make this prayer a regular habit in your life to keep the door of communication open with God.

LOCK 2: FAMILY DISHARMONY

Another block to prayer is family disharmony. God takes seriously how we interact with those in our family. We are commanded to honor our fathers and mothers, and God expects us to do so.

Is there anyone in your family whom you have failed to live with in an understanding way lately? How so?

What changes do you need to make today to better honor your closest relationships so that your prayers are not hindered?

Ask God for forgiveness and talk with God about a reconciliation plan. Write down at least two or three ways you hope to see God work in that relationship.

Commit your hopes to prayer. He is listening.

day 2

LOCKS, PART 2

LOCK 3: BABBLING WORDS

For many people, praying causes us to speak differently than how we speak at any other time. It causes us to repeat familiar phrases, offer bland statements, and appear more spiritual than what we may actually be.

Jesus warned against practicing our righteousness before men to be noticed by them (Matt. 6:1). If we parade our prayers in a way to gain man's approval, we might momentarily impress people, but we will not also receive God's approval or the answer to our prayers.

Look at the warning Jesus gives in Matthew 6:7-8. What hinders prayer and why is this important?

Let's make an important distinction. The religious elite in Jesus' day repeated special words or phrases in their prayers to get God's and others' attention. The words themselves had no real meaning. Jesus cautioned against this practice not because of the repetition of the prayers, but because the prayers were not authentic. Jesus makes it clear in Matthew 6:8 that prayer is a matter of the heart more so than a matter of words.

What promise does Jesus offer concerning the Father and prayer in Matthew 6:8? How will knowing this affect your prayer life?

LOCK 4: FAITHLESS REQUESTS

Another reason God does not answer our prayers is because we offer faithless requests. Sure we might pray to Him but our faith in His ability to answer those prayers is sadly minimal.

Do you believe that prayer is the most effective tool at your disposal? Why or why not?

Even the disciples, who walked with Jesus daily, did not fully grasp the power of prayer.

Read Mark 9:17-29 and note the word "believe." In this passage, a father asked Jesus' disciples to drive out a demon from his son, but they couldn't (v. 18).

See the father's honesty about his belief. Read Mark 9:24.

When the disciples asked Jesus why they were unable to cast out the demon, He answered that this demon would come out "by nothing but prayer." Prayer should always be our first response.

Read James 1:6-8 and list what hinders prayer and why it is important.

LOCK 5: REQUESTS CONTRARY TO GOD'S WILL

Read 1 John 5:14-15. What hinders prayer and why is this important?

Make no mistake about it—God's purpose will prevail (Prov. 19:21). We just have to learn how to pray according to His will. Read Romans 12:1-2. How do you understand what the will of God is? (Eph. 5:17)

God's Word reveals God's will. As we present ourselves to God, turn away from the backward values and vain thinking of the world, and allow Him to renew our minds, God's heart, desires, and good and perfect will become vividly clear to us. Then when we pray according to God's will, our prayers will become amazingly powerful and effective. (See Rom. 12:2.)

In our study this week, we have investigated to see if we are allowing things in our lives that might hinder our prayers. Though we all can "stumble in many ways" (James 3:2) we must take our relationship with a holy God seriously and deal with any issue that could hurt us spiritually. Knowing and loving God intimately is worth any sacrifice we need to make.

Take time to pray now. Confess any areas in your life that may be hindering your prayers and ask God to help you pursue His heart and overcome every one of these issues.

day 3

KEYS, PART 1

KEY 1: STAY CONSISTENT

Read Philippians 4:8-9. Why is it helpful to dwell on excellent things when anxiety and worry tend to grab your attention?

What are some excellent things you need to make it a habit to dwell upon?

In Philippians 4:7, Paul promised that the peace of God would guard the hearts of believers. In verses 8 and 9, Paul assured the Philippians that the God of peace would be with them. The peace of God only comes through the God of peace and His presence in our lives.

In the space below, be honest about what is causing you to be anxious. Fill out the columns to help get a perspective on your situation.

Concern	Is it Anxious-Worthy? (Phil. 4:6)	How to Pray	Verses to Pray

KEY 2: TRUST GOD'S CHARACTER

Anxiousness can be a practical sign of a theological problem. When we become anxious, we are refusing to acknowledge who God is and what God can do.

In the Sermon on the Mount, Jesus addressed how to deal with anxiety. His solution is not in the collection of more desires met. His solution is in confidence shown in God's faithfulness and loving care. Our peace does not come from what we have but in the One who has us.

Read Jesus' description of the cure for anxiety in Matthew 6:25-34.

Jesus described different things that can cause us to become anxious. Out of the things mentioned, what can cause the greatest anxiety within you?

How has God provided for you in the last year? Get specific.

When we trace God's hand in our lives, it helps us understand that we are not on our own. He is near and He is actively involved in our lives.

What does it mean to seek God's kingdom? His righteousness?

How does seeking these two things help us remove anxiety from our lives?

We do not seek God in order to acquire more stuff from Him. We seek Him in order to experience more of Him. When we seek Him and His righteousness, our focus shifts from the earthly realm to the heavenly, from possessions to His presence.

Every kingdom has a ruler. Seeking God's kingdom and having faith that He is in control and has authority over your life is a surefire way to eliminate worry.

In your time of prayer today, thank God for His provision in your life. Be honest about any needs that you have today. Don't just pray seeking answers for your concerns and desires. Ask Him to help you seek His kingdom and His righteousness first.

day 4

KEYS, PART 2

KEY 3: STRIVE FOR CONTENTMENT

In prayer, we must constantly perform a self-investigation to determine whether what we are asking for is a need or a want.

> **Read Paul's instruction to Timothy, his son in the faith, in 1 Timothy 6:6-10.**
>
> **What did Paul tell Timothy should be enough to make him content?**
>
> **Is anything causing discontentment in your life today? Is it a need or a want? Explain.**

With food and clothing, we should be content. Paul never described the type of food or the worth of the clothing. If we simply have those two things, we ought to be content. Paul is talking about our very basic needs.

> **Read Hebrews 13:5-6.**
>
> **Based on these verses, what do we have that will never be taken away from us?**

We are called to be satisfied with what we have. While that process can be difficult, here is the secret: Remember that God is your helper. We have the promise of His presence always. He is not a distant helper. He is intimately aware of all our cares and concerns. Jesus is our High Priest who stepped out of heaven to walk in flesh and He can sympathize with our weaknesses (Heb. 4:15). This is why the writer of Hebrews says:

> *Therefore let us approach the throne of grace with boldness, so that we may receive mercy and find grace to help us at the proper time.*
> **HEBREWS 4:16**

> **Today, in your time of prayer, focus on these things:**

1. God, make my soul content.
2. Thank You for what You have already given me.
3. Remind me of the sufficiency of Your presence in my life.

Approach God's throne with boldness today. He is ever present and ready to help at the proper time. His timeline doesn't always look like ours, but we can be assured that He will always provide.

KEY 4: MAKE A HABIT

Hopefully these practices you have learned will continue in your life far beyond this study, and these truths from God's Word are creating habits in your life that will change you forever!

Would you say prayer is a habit in your life? Why or why not?

What can you do today to make prayer a habit?

Read and be encouraged by the Scripture passages below concerning the power of prayer:

[14] . . . and My people who are called by My name humble themselves, pray and seek My face, and turn from their evil ways, then I will hear from heaven, forgive their sin, and heal their land. [15] My eyes will now be open and My ears attentive to prayer from this place.
2 CHRONICLES 7:14-15

The Lord is near all who call out to Him, all who call out to Him with integrity.
PSALM 145:18

day 5

PRAYER STRATEGY TARGET

Finally, today you get to put pen to paper on the Prayer Strategy Target.

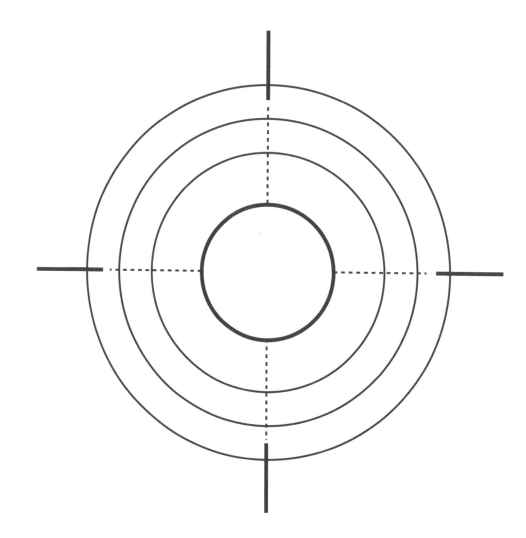

This week we will start filling in the slots around the target. You will notice that each target has 12 spaces to write and then one space to write in the bullseye. The bullseye is where you write the name of the persons for whom you are praying. But, around the names, you want to write what you are praying for them. Some of the spaces may stay the same from person to person. Other spaces will change for each person you are praying about. Today and the next few Prayer Strategy Days, we will talk about the specifics that you may pray about for everyone. We will give you a total of six ideas.

General Request #1: Pray that this person loves and obeys God.

If someone loves Jesus and obeys Him, so many other things will fall into place. "If you love Me, you will keep My commandments" (John 14:15). Obedience matters. Not in a legalistic way. Not as a means of pride or comparison with others. But life as a follower of Christ was never meant to be a casual attempt at doing as little as necessary—just enough to get by, just enough to feel good about going to the youth worship on Wednesday night. A person who is truly in Christ is steadily moving in a direction of greater obedience to Him.

A lifestyle of obedience—while not a condition that earns salvation—is a major key to answered prayer. Why should anyone call Jesus "Lord, Lord" if they're not serious about doing what He says? (Luke 6:46).

> *³ Everyone who has this hope fixed on Him purifies himself, just as He is pure …*
> *⁷ The one who practices righteousness is righteous, just as He is righteous.*
> **1 JOHN 3:3,7**

General Request #2: Pray that this person loves God's Word.

If you are praying for a person to fall in love with God, with God's Word and obey His commandments that are found there, then, you are praying a powerful prayer. There is nothing more important than loving God with all that we are. It is the greatest of all commandments and why we are here on the earth.

Pray that this person is open to the truth that can only be found in God's Word. Some people try to find a solid foundation for a sense of right from wrong apart from the Bible, but it is not possible. Pray that the person you're praying for will see that the Bible is exactly the foundation they are looking for. Pray they would have open hearts to hear and apply God's truth found in His Word.

WEEKLY SUMMARY

List below three things you learned this week about prayer and how you'll apply these to your life.

* *

* *

* *

NOTES

Use the space below to jot down any other thoughts or questions you have about prayer in general or what you've studied this past week.

SESSION 5

SPIRITUAL WARFARE

BATTLE PLAN |GROUP SESSION 5

SPIRITUAL WARFARE

We have a very real Savior. God's Word also reveals that we have a very real enemy and he has been using the same tactics against us from the very beginning. We must be scripturally and strategically able to respond to the enemy with spiritual warfare prayer.

OPENING WORD

Three volunteers will demonstrate this session's key concept with a fun exercise. Start by choosing who will play the part of "Joe/Jane the Christian." Then, blindfold Joe/Jane. Next, while Joe/Jane is blindfolded, choose two volunteers, one to be the "godly" voice in Joe/Jane's life and one to be the deceptive voice in Joe/Jane's life. The person speaking the "godly" voice will give him or her proper instructions on how to safely cross the room. The person speaking the deceiving voice, however, is more mischievous and should coach Joe/Jane directly into chairs and walls. It is up to Joe/Jane to get across the room by learning who to listen to and who to ignore.

STUDY THE SCRIPTURE: THE ENEMY'S SCHEMES:

What does God's Word teach us are the tricks Satan uses against us? He will...

* **Distract: Read Nehemiah 6:1-16.** How might the devil use distraction to keep us from obeying God? How are the enemy's distractions similar to how Nehemiah's enemies tried to distract him from obedience to God?

* **Deceive: Read John 8:42-45.** How is Satan described? What lies (about God, you, others, life) has he tried to convince you to believe?

* **Tempt: Read Ephesians 4:25-27.** What does it mean to give the devil an opportunity? How might bitterness, immorality, or rebellion be an opportunity? Can you think of one in your life right now?

* **Discourage: Read Joshua 1:9.** How does discouragement keep us from obeying God? Why would Satan want to discourage us? How does Satan attempt to discourage us?

* **Accuse: Read Zecharaiah 3:1-5.** How does Satan use accusation to attack us? How might he beat us down with accusation and guilt? Has this kind of attack been effective on you? Explain.

* **Divide: Read John 10:10.** How does division destroy our effectiveness and witness? How does Satan divide families? Churches? How have you seen him do this in or around your life?

STUDY THE SCRIPTURE: THE CHRISTIAN'S RESPONSE:

* **Resist, calling on Jesus' name: Read James 4:7-10.** According to verse 7, what happens when we resist Satan? Do most Christians live accordingly?

* **Take the way of escape: Read 1 Corinthians 10:13 and Matthew 6:13.** How does God provide escape from temptation?

* **Search for unconfessed sin: Read Psalm 139:23-24.** Why do we sometimes hesitate to pray this prayer?

* **Reclaim the ground from the enemy: Read Psalm 51:1-12.** Why is confession of sin so important in spiritual warfare?

* **Battle with Scripture: Read Matthew 4:1-11.** How did Jesus battle the temptations He faced? Why is Scripture so effective against temptation?

* **Name someone in targeted prayer: Read Ephesians 6:18.** How does praying for someone else help you in your personal spiritual battles?

* **Delight in the Lord: Read Philippians 4:4-7.** What happens in our hearts when we praise God and give Him our troubles?

WHAT DO I DO NOW?

Review the list of schemes and see if any of these things are at work in your life right now. Then, go through the list of Christian responses to see if you're actually applying them. Close by praying together that God will help you to discern the Devil's attacks on you and to stand firm and walk in victory over the enemy on a daily basis.

WHAT CAN I EXPECT?

In this coming week's devotions, we will learn how to put on the armor of God, and how to win the war over our thoughts.

day 1

IDENTIFYING THE ENEMY

To know how to pray in this battle, we must be aware of whom we are fighting.

We have a real Enemy. Our culture has made the Devil a comical costumed figure, but he is not an adversary who should be ignored or underestimated.

Satan is called the ruler of this world (John 16:11). He is described as exercising authority over the lower heavens, working in the lives of the disobedient (Eph. 2:2). Unbelievers are characterized as being held in the domain of darkness (Col. 1:13) by the power of Satan as he blinds their eyes so that they cannot see the light of the gospel (2 Cor. 4:3-4). He is the deceiver of the whole world as it is currently under his sway (1 John 5:19).

Satan uses windows of opportunity to steal, kill, and destroy (John 10:10). He approaches God in order to make accusations against us (Rev. 12:10). His original temptation caused Adam and Eve to doubt God's Word. He is bold enough to afflict righteous Job (Job 1:9-12), ask to sift Peter (Luke 22:31), torment Paul (2 Cor. 12:7), and tempt Jesus Himself (Luke 4:1,13).

Knowing this, do you think Satan is intimidated to engage you in battle? Are you aware of his schemes in your life? Explain.

In the Book of Revelation, Satan's demise is promised. Read the description in Revelation 12:7-12 and underline key phrases that describe Satan's actions and his end.

[7] Then war broke out in heaven: Michael and his angels fought against the dragon. The dragon and his angels also fought, [8] but he could not prevail, and there was no place for them in heaven

any longer. ⁹ So the great dragon was thrown out—the ancient serpent, who is called the Devil and Satan, the one who deceives the whole world. He was thrown to earth, and his angels with him.

¹⁰ Then I heard a loud voice in heaven say: The salvation and the power and the kingdom of our God and the authority of His Messiah have now come, because the accuser of our brothers has been thrown out: the one who accuses them before our God day and night. ¹¹ They conquered him by the blood of the Lamb and by the word of their testimony, for they did not love their lives in the face of death. ¹² Therefore rejoice, you heavens, and you who dwell in them! Woe to the earth and the sea, for the Devil has come down to you with great fury, because he knows he has a short time.

How does Satan try to deceive people today?

What might Satan use to accuse you before God?

What two things are given to us to be able to conquer him (v. 11)?

In your prayer time today, thank Jesus for His blood that silences the accusations of the deceiver. Your testimony of God's grace in your life sends the enemy packing!

When Satan reminds you of what you have done, remind him of what Christ has done. Spend time thanking Jesus for salvation and praying against the enemy's lying, scheming, deceiving ways in your life and the lives of those around you. Pray for discernment to see how he is attacking you and for courage to stand firm in your faith.

day 2

ARE YOU ON SATAN'S RADAR?

In yesterday's homework, we identified the real enemy. We know about Satan. But here's a question for you: Does Satan know about you? Are you even on Satan's radar?

Read Acts 19:11-17 and underline key phrases as you read.

God was performing extraordinary miracles by Paul's hands, ¹² so that even facecloths or work aprons that had touched his skin were brought to the sick, and the diseases left them, and the evil spirits came out of them.

¹³ Then some of the itinerant Jewish exorcists attempted to pronounce the name of the Lord Jesus over those who had evil spirits, saying, "I command you by the Jesus that Paul preaches!" ¹⁴ Seven sons of Sceva, a Jewish chief priest, were doing this. ¹⁵ The evil spirit answered them, "I know Jesus, and I recognize Paul—but who are you?" ¹⁶ Then the man who had the evil spirit leaped on them, overpowered them all, and prevailed against them, so that they ran out of that house naked and wounded. ¹⁷ This became known to everyone who lived in Ephesus, both Jews and Greeks. Then fear fell on all of them, and the name of the Lord Jesus was magnified.

In this passage, God was doing amazing things through the hands of Paul. Some traveling Jewish ministers were also attempting to exorcise demons from people.

When they tried to use the name of Jesus in their ministry, what did the demon say to them? What does this imply?

What did the demon do to them?

What does this passage teach us about winning spiritual battles?

The demons obviously knew about Jesus, but they were also fully aware of a missionary named Paul. He had done enough damage to their kingdom to get their attention.

But these seven sons of Sceva? They weren't even on the radar. No memos were posted about their lives. No concerns about their power.

They attempted to use the name of Jesus to perform miracles, but the evil spirit knew they did not belong to Christ. And without the power of Christ on their side, there was no hope that their ministry would succeed.

It begs the question: *Do the forces of hell know me by name?*

What are you doing to push back against Satan's forces?

Are you acting on your own strength or relying on the authority of Christ?

Spend time in prayer today, asking God to empower you in spiritual battles. Ask Him to keep your eyes alert to the enemy around you, and give you power and boldness so that you can stand firm against the tactics of the Devil (Eph. 6:11).

day 3

THE ARMOR OF GOD

To be able to fight well in spiritual warfare, we must rely on the teachings of Scripture and on the One who lives in us who is greater than the one who is in the world.

Paul teaches that to fight spiritual battles, we must put on the armor of God.

Read Ephesians 6:10-17. Why do we put on the armor of God (v. 11)?

What are we at war with in this life (v.12)?

Keep in mind that putting on the armor of God is not a battlefield technique, but a preparation technique. Paul urges believers to take on the full armor of God in order to be prepared for the day of battle. Then we will be able to stand strong. Don't wait until the battle is raging to gird yourself with the protection of the armor of God.

Let's take a look at this armor in more detail. There are six pieces of armor named in verses 14-17. List each one, describing what these items are to look like in your life.

Which piece of armor are you employing the most right now? Is there a weak place in your armor that you need the Lord to strengthen?

Following the list of armor, Paul adds an essential element to our success in spiritual warfare. Read Ephesians 6:18-20 and answer the questions that follow.

We are commanded to pray throughout the entire battle. What does Paul mean when he says to pray "in the Spirit?"

To pray in the Spirit is to be inspired, and led to pray by God's Holy Spirit (Rom. 8:14-16). When we are right with the Lord and surrendered to Him, His Spirit will fill us and lead us to cry out to God and pray for specific things and to pray specific verses back to God. (Read Rom. 8:26-27.)

What did Paul ask the people to pray for concerning him (v. 19-20)?

After explaining how to put on the armor of God to prepare for battle against the Enemy, Paul asked for prayers for boldness. The same missionary who penned the words, "I am not ashamed of the gospel" (Rom. 1:16) still asked for others to pray for him so that he could fight well in the battle. He also asked for people to pray that God would open doors to share the gospel with others (Col. 4:3). He was rallying prayer support so that he could fight against the schemes of the Devil in his life and in his ministry.

If Paul asked others to pray that for him, why wouldn't we pray that for ourselves? We all have shared prayer requests before—we pray for the sick, for jobs, for family, or those who have lost a loved one. These things are wonderful and needed topics of prayer. But how often do we ask for people to pray for us that we would be bold in sharing the gospel?

Who in your life needs to hear the gospel?

Who can you ask to pray for you that you would be bold to share the gospel?

Contact them today.

Contacting prayer warriors to pray for you not only provides prayer support but also accountability. Send out those messages and then pray that God will open up a door for you to share
with boldness.

day 4
TAKE EVERY THOUGHT CAPTIVE

Begin today by reading 2 Corinthians 10:3-5 and make notes of important phrases or words.

What phrases or words grabbed your attention and why?

What do you think it means to take "every thought captive to obey Christ"?

Just like the spiritual battles we fight are unseen, some of our most difficult struggles are inside our own minds: pride, insecurity, lust, fear, distrust, doubt, worry. Sometimes not even our family or closest friends know our deepest, most troubling thoughts. But the Lord knows.

Read Hebrews 4:12-13.

The Word of God is the tool to know if our heart is in line with His, to know if our thoughts are under His authority. We cannot take up physical arms to fight spiritual battles. We must learn to fight these battles on our knees. Through the weapon of prayer, we can demolish internal strongholds—lies Satan tells us to separate us from God's truth.

What kinds of strongholds could Satan be attempting to establish in your life?

What kinds of strongholds could Satan be attempting to establish in the lives of those closest to you?

The struggles are real. Instead of testing out all physical options, attempting frivolous arguments, or garnering all the professional help we can find, have we honestly prayed that the dominion of darkness would be thwarted? Have we prayed for these strongholds to be broken down in the name of Jesus? Remember, prayer is not our last line of defense, it is our only line of defense.

Read James 4:7. According to this verse, what is the solution for spiritual victory over the Devil?

Finish your time today by praying for spiritual victories over these spiritual strongholds. Submit to God in prayer and ask Him to take captive every thought so that you may be fully obedient to Him. Lift up the words of the final petition of Jesus' model prayer:

And do not bring us into temptation, but deliver us from the evil one.
MATTHEW 6:13

day 5

PRAYER STRATEGY TARGET

We will continue our Prayer Strategy Day today talking about a few other general requests that you can pray over any person regardless of where they are in their life. Last week we hit:

General Request #1: Pray that this person loves and obeys God.

General Request #2: Pray that this person follows God's commands.

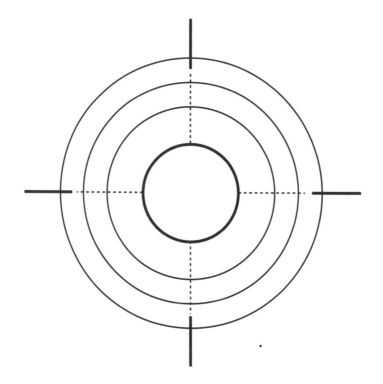

Today we will look at two more requests.

General Request #3: Pray that this person will love and serve others.

Consider 1 Peter 4:8-11:

> *[8] Above all, love each other deeply, because love covers over a multitude of sins. [9] Offer hospitality to one another without grumbling. [10] Each of you should use whatever gift you have received to serve others, as faithful stewards of God's grace in its various forms. [11] If anyone speaks, they should do so as one who speaks the very words of God. If anyone serves, they should do so with the strength God provides, so that in all things God may be praised through Jesus Christ. To him be the glory and the power for ever and ever. Amen. (NIV)*

"Above all, love each other deeply." What a challenge. It isn't always easy, but what a payoff if we do. We should be known by our love for one another. So as you are praying, pray that this person would love and serve others.

General Request #4: Pray that this person will have faith instead of doubt.

When you pray, you should rest in the fact that God is not unaware, unable, uncaring, unwilling, or unlikely to answer. That's why He keeps prompting you to ask in faith. Your heart can be right with God and with others, and yet your doubts during prayer can create roadblocks.

Peter, for example, unnecessarily denied Jesus three times. Sometimes we, too, might quietly deny God's faithfulness, goodness, or ability in our hearts when we approach Him. This lack of faith will clog up your prayer life. You'll quit wanting to come close to God if you don't trust Him or believe He is good.

So, when you are praying for others, pray that they would trust in God's faithfulness. That they would take Him at His word and believe that He understands their needs and is able to help.

Next week, on Day 5, we will look at the final two characteristics of what we can pray for others.

WEEKLY SUMMARY

List below three things you learned this week about prayer and how you'll apply these to your life.

       *

       *

       *

NOTES

Use the space below to jot down any other thoughts or questions you have about prayer in general or what you've studied this past week.

PRAYING
IN FAITH

BATTLE PLAN | GROUP SESSION 6

PRAYING IN FAITH

When you pray, do you really believe that God is going to work on your behalf? Why would God teach us so much about prayer unless He wanted us to pray to Him and wanted to answer our prayers? But He commands us to pray in faith. There is a great way to petition the Lord and invite heaven to earth—praying in faith!

OPENING WORD

Encourage your fellow group members to share their answers to these questions:

* What would happen if the cheerleading coach and the football coach switched jobs for a day?
* Describe how your church's Christmas production would turn out if a first grader directed it.
* Do you give driving directions to people in cities you have never even visited? Why or why not?
* Would you ask your 5 year old sibling for help on your math homework? Why not, exactly?
* We place our faith in people who are experienced and accomplished in their fields. We ask for advice from experts, not newbies. When we receive coaching from a pro, we can confidently place our faith in it. On an eternally higher level, we can absolutely trust in God's ability, wisdom, and will when we pray. He foreknows our prayers, has a perfect track record of answering, and invites us to pray.

STUDY THE SCRIPTURE: READ HEBREWS 4:14-16

PRAY WITH CONFIDENCE.

* When we go to Jesus for strength to stand up under temptation, what gives Him the ability to understand what we are going through?
* What does the invitation to draw near to God reveal about Him? What kind of relationship does God want with us?
* Does this verse help you to trust God more? Does it make you want to pray with greater confidence? Why or why not?

STUDY THE SCRIPTURE: READ MATTHEW 21:18-22

PRAY BELIEVING

* What, according to Jesus' words in verse 21, did the disciples have to do in order to see greater miracles than the withering fig tree?
* Jesus told His disciples that they could even order mountains to be cast into the sea. Does that challenge your prayer life? Do you believe God can do impossible things? Why or why not?

* What is the key word in verse 22 and why does it matter? Does that mean this if you believe hard enough, God will always, immediately give you whatever you want? Explain.

STUDY THE SCRIPTURE: READ JAMES 1:5-8
PRAY WITHOUT DOUBTING

* What is the major "no-no" when praying for wisdom?
* How does this passage describe the person who prays for wisdom while doubting? Why?
* Why is doubting such a problem to our prayer life?
* How is doubting God's power or goodness kind of like saying, "I don't really trust you God?"

STUDY THE SCRIPTURE: READ EPHESIANS 3:11-21
PRAY BOLDLY

* What does this passage teach us about God's love and His power?
* When we are confident in God's strength and goodness, believe that He is able, and cast doubt to the side, what kinds of prayers are we going to pray?
* What is your favorite word in verse 12 and why?
* According to v. 20, what is God able to do? Does your prayer life reflect that truth? Why or why not?

WHAT DO I DO NOW?

Consider and discuss: How does thanking God for things He's done in the past help us to pray with greater faith toward the future?

As a group, pray a prayer that honors the combined message of these passages. Implementing the structure of the Lord's prayer, let the first words of your prayer address God according to the Ephesians 3:20 description of Him. As you pray, know that God is already aware of your group's needs and what you are going to pray and can start answering even before you ask.

WHAT CAN I EXPECT?

Jesus taught us to open our prayers addressing God as our Father. This coming week's devotions will explore ways in which God is able to deliver us, concerned with what concerns us, and forgiving. We will also use the Prayer Strategy Target to learn about praying in the Holy Spirit.

day 1

OUR FATHER IS ABLE

Understanding the identity of our Father is a foundational principle concerning prayer.

God's Word is the best source to remedy our inadequate understanding concerning our Heavenly Father. This week, we will counteract common misconceptions concerning God. The more we understand God's character and how He interacts with His children, the more confident we will be in our prayers.

MISCONCEPTION #1: GOD IS UNABLE

Let's continue to study what God's Word says about our Heavenly Father.

Under each verse, make notes about what it teaches concerning the character of God. Pray as you go through these Scriptures. You don't want to just gather knowledge of God without deepening your relationship with HIm. Keep praying.

*Yet for us there is one God, the Father. All things
are from Him, and we exist for Him.*
1 CORINTHIANS 8:6A

While this verse clearly tells us that all things are from God, what are some specific things He has given you? List those below and thank God for them.

When the Scripture says, "we exist for Him," what does that mean practically for your life? How does that affect the way you approach family, friends, school, extracurricular activities, etc.? Commit those areas of your life to Him in prayer.

One God and Father of all, who is above all and through all and in all.
EPHESIANS 4:6

Your Father is above all. In what ways are you thankful for this aspect of God?

He is able to do all things because He is above all things. Praise Him for His sovereignty and authority.

Praise the God and Father of our Lord Jesus Christ, who has blessed us in Christ with every spiritual blessing in the heavens.
EPHESIANS 1:3

What are the spiritual blessings with which God has blessed you? List them below and thank your Father for these gifts (forgiveness of sins, spiritual gifts, etc.).

Close in prayer by thanking your generous Father for who He is and what He has done. He is the only God. All things come from Him and exist for Him. He is above all things. He has blessed us with every spiritual blessing. Thank Him that He is able to do above and beyond anything we could ask or think (Eph. 3:20).

day 2

OUR FATHER IS CARING

MISCONCEPTION #2: GOD IS UNCARING

Many people interpret negative circumstances in their lives incorrectly, believing God does not care enough about them to get involved. Scripture paints a completely different picture of our Father.

Children want to be able to trust that their parents will continually care for them—that they will come through in their time of greatest need. You may or may not be able to say that about your earthly father, but you can be confident in the steadfastness of your Heavenly Father. Today, we are going to thank God for His consistency and care in our lives.

Read Psalm 68:5 and note how the psalmist describes our Father.

Holy means *set apart*. It is different. Better. Special. Unique. This verse tells us that God has a set apart dwelling place. It is a place where He chooses and desires to dwell (Ps. 68:16). Many people think God is unaware of their everyday lives. Believing that He is too lofty or out-of-touch with us down here on earth, some people will live in such a way that ignores God's involvement in their lives. They ignore God because they believe God is ignoring them. Yet even from His holy place, God cares for those in need.

From His holy dwelling, for what two groups of people does God show concern according to Psalm 68:5?

What does that teach us about His character?

The Bible teaches us that God knows how many hairs are on our heads (Luke 12:7), He collects our tears in a bottle (Ps. 56:8), and He promises to supply all of our needs (Phil. 4:19). God is not unaware; He is not uncaring.

Read Isaiah 64:8 and notice how aware and involved God is in your life.

*Yet L*ORD*, You are our Father; we are the clay, and You are*
our potter; we all are the work of Your hands.
ISAIAH 64:8

God has created you and sustained you in a unique way. He has written every one of your days down in a book before anyone else had a chance to crack open the cover.

> **Thank God for how He has created you and how He has sustained you. Before moving on, take time to praise Him for how He fearfully and wonderfully made you (Ps. 139:14).**

> **Read Matthew 7:9-11. How is our heavenly Father compared to our earthly fathers in this passage?**

James also reminds believers about the greater nature of gifts given by God compared to the lesser value of offerings given by the world.

> **Read James 1:17.**

> *Every generous act and every perfect gift is from above, coming down from*
> *the Father of lights; with Him there is no variation or shadow cast by turning.*
> **JAMES 1:17**

> **What are three generous acts or perfect gifts that God has given you?**
> **1.**
> **2.**
> **3.**

> **What does it mean that there is "no variation" with our Father?**

Thank God for His care and awareness in your life. Be honest with Him concerning your needs, acknowledging that He is near and available to help. What is your greatest care today? Cast it on your loving Father and eagerly wait to see how He responds.

day 3

OUR FATHER IS CONCERNED

MISCONCEPTION #3: GOD IS UNCONCERNED

While some people struggle with the idea that God is unaware of our difficult situations, many people struggle in a different way. Some believe that God is unconcerned with our choices. If we believe God to be too distant or too soft to concern Himself with our lifestyle, we can slip into complacency and unholy living.

Make no mistake—God is not mocked (Gal. 6:7). He is concerned with your situation, but He is also concerned with your lifestyle.

Note how our Father is described in Deuteronomy 32:6.

Is this how you repay the LORD, you foolish and senseless people? Isn't He your Father and Creator? Didn't He make you and sustain you?
DEUTERONOMY 32:6

In this passage, the people of God were not acting like the people of God. They were foolish and senseless in their decisions and this type of thinking was leading them to live unholy lives. The absurdity of their actions was pitted against the character of God. How could the people act like this if they had such a caring Father?

What is important about God being our Father that should cause us to think carefully about how we live?

God is not only concerned with how we live, but He is a Father who cares enough that He will step in and stop us when we go too far. He is a Father who disciplines His children.

Read Hebrews 12:9-11 and discover something about the concerned nature of our Father.

⁹ Furthermore, we had natural fathers discipline us, and we respected them. Shouldn't we submit even more to the Father of spirits and live? ¹⁰ For they disciplined us for a short time based on what seemed good to them, but He does it for our benefit, so that we can share His holiness. ¹¹ No discipline seems enjoyable at the time, but painful. Later on, however, it yields the fruit of peace and righteousness to those who have been trained by it.
HEBREWS 12:9-11

What methods did your parents use to discipline you?

Even though it was difficult to receive, what benefit did you gain from their discipline?

How do you think God disciplines us? What methods does He use?

What is God's goal in disciplining us?

God's wrath is designated for unbelievers. God's discipline is designated for believers. The way to avoid wrath is to receive Christ. The way to avoid discipline is to obey Christ.

Pray and ask God if there are some things He wants you to stop doing or start doing. Commit these items to Him in prayer and submit to your loving Heavenly Father.

day 4

OUR FATHER IS FORGIVING

MISCONCEPTION #4: GOD IS UNFORGIVING

We sometimes imagine God to be as petty as we are. Assuming He holds grudges due to our previous mistakes, sometimes our prayers are stifled because we believe He doesn't want to hear from us.

While our Father is diligent to discipline us, He is also eager to pardon us. He loves to show compassion to His children. Do you remember the parable of the Prodigal Son?

The younger son asked for his part of his inheritance and squandered it in "foolish living" (Luke 15:13). When he hit rock bottom and came to his senses, he reasoned to himself: "I'll get up, go to my father, and say to him, 'Father, I have sinned against heaven and in your sight. I'm no longer worthy to be called your son. Make me like one of your hired hands" (Luke 15:18-19).

As he made the long and humbling trip back home, can you imagine the scenarios that ran through his mind?

How could this young man's father have responded?

Willing to accept the consequences and assume a demoted role with his father, he went home. But instead of condemnation and speeches filled with "I told you so's," read how this father reacted in Luke 15:20.

> *So he got up and went to his father. But while the son was still a long way off, his father saw him and was filled with compassion. He ran, threw his arms around his neck, and kissed him.*
> **LUKE 15:20**

What words surprise you in this verse? Why?

This father was eagerly longing for his son's return. Seeing him from afar, this father, filled with compassion, didn't just walk to his son. He ran to him! Overwhelmed with joy, he passionately threw his arms around his son's neck and showered him with kisses.

This is not a picture of an unforgiving, detached father. This is a picture of our Father in heaven who longs for our return and rejoices when we come to our senses.

How does this image change the way you view your Heavenly Father?

As the nation of Israel emerged from 40 years of wilderness wanderings, Moses reminded the people of how God had persevered with them. See how God is portrayed among the people of Israel before they entered the promised land:

> *30 The LORD your God who goes before you will fight for you, just as you saw Him do for you in Egypt. 31 And you saw in the wilderness how the LORD your God carried you as a man carries his son all along the way you traveled until you reached this place.*
> **DEUTERONOMY 1:30-31**

What is so encouraging in this depiction of our Father?

Today, spend time thanking our Father for running to us with compassion. Thank Him for fighting for us when all our strength is gone. Thank Him for the way He carried us to this point in our lives. Spend time expressing your love and gratitude to our Father.

day 5

PRAYER STRATEGY TARGET

Before we continue our Prayer Strategy Target work, let's recall the 4 general requests we discussed previously:

General Request #1: Pray that this person loves and obeys God.

General Request #2: Pray that this person follows God's commands.

General Request #3: Pray that this person will love and serve others.

General Request #4: Pray that this person will have faith instead of doubt.

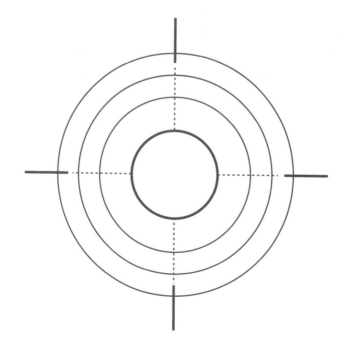

Now, we move to the last two general characteristics. Remember, though, these are not the only things you need to pray for people. But hopefully, these will get you started.

General Request #5: Pray for the fruit of the Spirit to be manifested in this person's life.

²² But the fruit of the Spirit is love, joy, peace, forbearance, kindness, goodness, faithfulness, ²³ gentleness and self-control. Against such things there is no law. ²⁴ Those who belong to Christ Jesus have crucified the flesh with its passions and desires. ²⁵ Since we live by the Spirit, let us keep in step with the Spirit. (NIV)

GALATIANS 5:22-25

These qualities and characteristics flow out of a person who is connected to God. These are what God produces in a person who follows after Him. Pray that the person would stay connected to the Lord and that this fruit would flow freely in his/her life. Pray that the person would have peace through Christ Jesus. Pray that the person would have self-control in his/her life. Pray that the life of this person is marked by kindness and goodness. This is what God wants for each believer, so pray it along with Him!

General Request#6: Pray the Lord's Prayer over this person.

As you think about how to really target this kind of praying, consider a strategy that actually works for all kinds of different settings and different people: using the Lord's Prayer as an outline. Instead of praying it for yourself, pray it for your fellow believers. Something like this:

Father in Heaven, I pray for my brother (my sister), praising Your name for them, asking You to fill their heart with worship for You today. Help them to honor Your name above themselves. May their primary desire always be to advance Your kingdom, wherever they happen to be, whatever they happen to be doing.

May they align themselves on the earth with Your will, just as surely as Your will is followed and accomplished in heaven. Provide them, I pray, with their daily bread—with everything You know is required for them to thrive and be cared for. And grant them repentance, forgiving them of their sins—even as You forgive me of mine—while also keeping their relationships free from bitterness and difficulty as they forgive those who've sinned against them.

Please, Lord, protect them from temptation, from allowing them to be overloaded with adversity. And deliver them from all evil—from every scheme and attack of the enemy, from every weapon intended to defeat and discourage them. For Yours, Lord, is the kingdom, the power, the glory, forever. You reign and rule and have already given them victory through the finished work of Christ. So I pray for them today, and I pray in His name, amen.

Now that's strategically targeting a prayer. That's biblical praying. That's using the Word—and where appropriate, using your specific knowledge of the person—to aim a prayer in such a way that it covers all aspects of their life and seeks God's will for that person.

WEEKLY SUMMARY

List below three things you learned this week about prayer and how you'll apply these to your life.

> *

> *

> *

NOTES

Use the space below to jot down any other thoughts or questions you have about prayer in general or what you've studied this past week.

PRAYING SPECIFICALLY & STRATEGICALLY

BATTLE PLAN |GROUP SESSION 7

PRAYING SPECIFICALLY AND STRATEGICALLY

God wants to answer our prayers. He is glorified and reveals more of His kindness, love, and provision when we pray and He responds in power. But we should learn to pray like those in the Bible whose prayers were answered. They persistently prayed according to the Word of God, the will of God, and with great faith. But they also learned to pray specifically. Christians often pray generic and vague prayers. This may be a way of avoiding disappointment if God seemingly does not provide the specific thing for which they prayed. Christians often pray sporadically and infrequently. So, they see sporadic and infrequent results. May you and your church group aspire to be believers who pray specifically and strategically.

OPENING WORD

Play a quick single round of charades with your whole group acting as a team. Choose a volunteer. Use current movie or book titles for the volunteer to choose from. After you play one round, discuss these questions:

* The charade performer gave specific instructions toward a specific word or phrase. How frustrating would it have been for everyone to just ignore those instructions? Would it be a little like praying to God in a way that completely disregards His instructions in the Bible?

* The person did not speak, but wanted the group to speak to him or her. In what ways is that like prayer? Just as the person was looking for a specifc answer, is God wanting us to pray specific prayers? What do you think are the greatest benefits of being specific in our praying to God?

STUDY THE SCRIPTURE: PRAYING SPECIFICALLY AND STRATEGICALLY

If your heart is right and you are ready to pray, what should you pray for? Here are seven things that can help inspire and guide you to pray more specifically.

* **Pray for the needs of the moment: Read Matthew 6:11.** Why did Jesus not instruct us to pray for tomorrow's bread as well? What do you or the people in your life need TODAY? Let that guide what you ask for in prayer.

* **Pray that god's heavenly will is done: Read Matthew 6:9-10.** Heaven is perfect. So, what are we really saying when we ask God to have His perfect heavenly will done in an earthly situation? What would Jesus be praying for in our situation?

* **Pray in accordance with your gifts: Read Romans 12:4-8.** How might your passions, strengths, and spiritual giftedness shape how you pray? How might someone who is gifted in mercy pray differently from someone gifted in service or teaching? Let this expand how you pray.

* **Pray scripture: Read 1 John 5:14.** Why is it important that we pray according to God's Word? By personalizing a passage, we can use God's Word to expand how we pray. For example, Psalm 91 helps us pray for protection. Ephesians 1 and 3 shows us how to pray for spiritual understanding.

* **Pray according to the names of God: Read Psalm 116:13.** Lead students to look up the following names of God on their mobile devices and have them share what they discovered.

Jehovah-Jireh	Jehovah-Shalom
El-Olam	Jehovah-Rapha
Immanuel	El Shaddai

How does knowing God's names and what they mean help us pray more effectively?

* **Pray according to God's glory: Read 2 Corinthians 4:6.** When we invite God to bring glory to Himself through even the worst of situations, how does that change our perspective of the situation?

* **Pray according to God's spirit: Read Romans 8:26-28.** Interceding is praying on someone's behalf. What does v. 26 teach us about the Spirit? How might God's Spirit help guide how we pray?

WHAT DO I DO NOW?

* Review the seven mentioned aspects of praying specifically and strategically. Which of these are you using already to help your prayer life? Which ones can you start to utilize? Discuss with the group how to better use all of these for effective praying.

* Close in prayer as a group and pray specifically for one another's needs and for God to be glorified in your situations.

WHAT CAN I EXPECT?

This week's devotions will help you know better how to be strategic and specific in your praying.

day 1
PRAYING SCRIPTURE

There is power packed into God's Word. Unfortunately, for many of us, the practice of blending prayer with the reading of Scripture remains unexplored.

If your heart is right with God and others and you are ready to pray, then what should guide your praying? True, prayer can flow directly from your heart. No script is necessary. Nothing prescribed or recited. Prayer is personal. Completely unique. Yet even with this much freedom involved, God does provide powerful resources to help us pray strategically and specifically. These will help you know for certain that your heart is beating in step with God's.

Perhaps the first and most comprehensive guide is to pray using the very words He's already spoken in His Word. We humans are fickle. Hot and cold. Moods and emotions that flame within us today can be nearly forgotten memories by the end of the week. But when we pray with words and thoughts that are inspired by Scripture, we're assured that our praying is anchored in bedrock truths that stretch back centuries. They keep our praying steadfast and consistent.

You may think, , "Well, I don't know the Bible enough. I wouldn't know where to start." That is not a problem, you can even pray about that too. God will guide you as you seek Him.

Praying God's Word means reading or reciting Scripture in an attitude and spirit of prayer. We let the meaning of the verses become our prayer. These scriptural prayers encourage, inspire, and transform our minds and hearts.

> **Instead of picking verses randomly, we have listed several Scripture prayers. First, read them and summarize the context and content of each one.**
>
> **Acts 4:24-30**
>
> **Philippians 1:9-11**

Colossians 1:9-14

1 Thessalonians 3:11-13

Hebrews 13:20-21

Revelation 4:8,11

Revelation 5:9-10

Which one of these prayers speaks most closely to your current situation?

What jumps out as especially relevant to you? Why?

Write down the passage again as a prayer and dwell on each word and its meaning.

Does this prayer lead you to pray other prayers of confession, repentance, or praise? Are you challenged to pursue a new act of obedience? Explain.

How will you make this spiritual discipline of praying Scripture a part of your regular prayer life?

See, that wasn't too difficult, was it? If you start to put praying Scripture into practice, it will bear much fruit in your life.

Pray and ask God to prompt you with specific verses to pray at specific times. Ask Him to empower you with His Spirit and help you to pray in faith and trust His Word as you go through your day.

day 2

PRAYING GOD'S NAMES

Dr. John Smith is called different names at different times. His father calls him "Son"; his wife calls him "Sweetheart"; his patients call him "Doc"; and his friends at church call him "Brother Jack." At the hospital he's "the doctor with the best bedside manner," and the waiters at a local restaurant refer to him as "that happy Christian who leaves good tips." John isn't multiple people. He's one man with multiple roles and character traits.

Each of John's names or titles reveals a little more about who he is, what he does, and how he relates to others. In like manner, the Bible reveals that our one God has many names. When we pray to Him, we may come to Him for a wide variety of reasons. Because He is eternal and limitless, the many titles and descriptions used of Him in the Bible are vast and astounding. But that's the point. Each name of God helps us to understand, value, and worship Him even more.

We are going to explore just a few of God's many names today and discuss how to pray using the names of God as our foundation. Psalm 91:1–2 states, "He who dwells in the secret place of the Most High shall abide under the shadow of the Almighty. I will say of the Lord, 'He is my refuge and my fortress; My God, in Him I will trust'" (NKJV). In these two verses, the same God is referred to by multiple names and descriptions: Elyon (the Most High), Shaddai (the Almighty), Yahweh (the Lord), my refuge, my fortress, and my God (Elohim).

> **As you consider each of these names and descriptions below, make notes about the significance of each one based upon Psalm 91:1-2.**
>
> 1. **Elyon (the Most High):**
>
> 2. **Shaddai (the Almighty):**

3. **Yahweh (the Lord):**

4. **Elohim (my refuge or fortress):**

Yesterday we discussed praying God's Word. Today we are discussing the names of God. Let's combine the two together. Below we've listed some names of God and some Scripture references. Look up the Scripture passage identified for each name and write a prayer to God thanking him for this particular attribute. Note why this one is meaningful to you.

1. **The Eternal God - Isaiah 40:28**

2. **The God of All Comfort - 2 Corinthians 1:3**

3. **The King of Heaven - Daniel 4:37**

4. **The Lord of Peace - 2 Thessalonians 3:16**

5. **The Light of the World - John 8:12**

These are just a few of the names of God and Jesus in the Bible. Even if you don't remember any formal or Hebrew names of God, you can praise Him in your native language by calling out to Him as the God of love, faithfulness, mercy, comfort, protection, justice, forgiveness, power, and salvation. The list goes on and on.

The point is to seek Him, worship Him, and pray to Him for who He is. To acknowledge Him as the Creator, Your Father, and the One who is everything you need. His love for you is great, and your love for Him is reflected by your desire to know Him and obey Him.

So as you pray strategically, remember to call out to your God by His names as you learn them. He loves to hear His children acknowledge Him for all He does and all He can do. And doesn't He deserve it? After all, He is God our Salvation. "Let them praise the name of the LORD: for his name alone is excellent; his glory is above the earth and heaven" (Ps. 148:13, KJV).

Pick out one of the verses from today. Meditate on that passage today—write it out, memorize it, think about it. Use that verse as you pray today, thanking God for who He is.

day 3

PRAYING OFFENSIVELY

Part of a good prayer strategy is knowing how to pray against evil. We all know, of course, the dangers that lurk within temptation. We're well familiar with the enemy's arrows of fear, anger, lust and jealousy. But today we will focus on going on the offensive in a positive way, praying for the advancement of love, life, and truth.

Sure, there are times when we need to play defense. But not all the time. We need a game plan for offense as well—asking God to open doors for the gospel, to send forth laborers into the harvest field, to pour out His Holy Spirit in revival, to fill us with His love and the knowledge of His will, to use our spiritual gifts in His service, and to raise up a generation who will honor His name. Spiritual warfare is about standing our ground against the enemy and taking new ground for the kingdom.

Let your light shine before men in such a way that they may see
your good works and glorify your Father who is in heaven.

MATTHEW 5:16

Think of a particular friend or family member as you go through these questions:

What is the most loving thing you could request for them right now?

What are you praying for this person that has eternal significance?

How can you pray for this person to advance God's kingdom?

How can you pray for this person in a way that would bring glory to God?

We find positive prayers and steps for taking ground all through Scripture. In fact, God wants to help us and give us gifts along the way to encourage and assist us. Jesus tells us in Matthew 7:11, "If you then, being evil, know how to give good gifts to your children, how much more will your Father who is in heaven give what is good to those who ask Him!"

When we love someone, we want nothing but the best for them. John prays this type of prayer in 3 John 2, saying, "Beloved, I pray that in all respects you may prosper and be in good health, just as your soul prospers." If God is good and is preparing good things for us, then we need to be actively seeking and asking for these things.

Pray loving prayers. We need to cover situations in prayer and ask God to bless, provide, and be glorified as much as possible . . . praying that He would do more than we can ask or imagine. Why? Because His glory is the ultimate goal of all praying.

We need to pray bold prayers for our friends and family. Prayers that have eternal significance. While we want them to be safe and satisfied with life, we need to be praying they will make a difference in the world for Christ, that God would call them out for service in His kingdom and they would accept that call.

Don't just pray against hardships, pray for the positive to happen. Instead of praying that your church leaders won't fight during a business meeting, pray for loving unity and revival to break out, resulting in greater ministry opportunities.

Romans 12:21 says, "Do not be overcome by evil, but overcome evil with good." The apostle Paul was a great example of this mind-set when praying for his new brothers and sisters in the faith. He wrote in long, uplifting terms in Colossians 1:9–12, "We have not ceased to pray for you and to ask that you may be filled with the knowledge of His will in all spiritual wisdom and understanding, so that you will walk in a manner worthy of the Lord, to please Him in all respects, bearing fruit in every good work and increasing in the knowledge of God; strengthened with all power, according to His glorious might, for the attaining of all steadfastness and patience; joyously giving thanks to the Father, who has qualified us to share in the inheritance of the saints in Light."

Wouldn't you want something prayed over you like that? To be filled with knowledge, wisdom, and an understanding of God's will? To bear much fruit in your life for God's glory?

This is how to pray proactively and go on the offense. Pray for someone right now in your family. Ask for God's richest blessings upon their life.

day 4

PRAYING PREEMPTIVELY

If you were the leader of a country and discovered that you would soon be attacked by a brutal, invading army, what would you do? If no terms of peace were possible, you would do everything plausible to quickly prepare for war. Gathering resources. Stationing troops.

This is also what we must do in prayer. We must first fight our battles on our knees before the battle rages in the natural realm. Let's spend some time today looking at the enemy's playbook so we can be preemptive in our prayer strategy.

DISTRACTION

Misdirection is Warfare 101. David wrote, "I am restless in my complaint and am surely distracted, because of the voice of the enemy" (Ps. 55:2–3). Satan will constantly try to get you off track. To focus on even good things which are not God's best things.

> **In what areas of your life are you prone to distraction? Spend a moment writing a prayer out to the Lord about focusing on God's best.**

DECEPTION

Jesus said whenever Satan speaks a lie (which is all the time), "he speaks from his own nature, for he is a liar and the father of lies" (John 8:44). Strongholds, addictions, and sins are founded upon lies. They are a perversion of God's truth. Promises never delivered. False advertising.

Sin will fail you, let you down, and leave you empty. But Satan's temptations brazenly try to assure you that if you act now, your situation will be different. It won't affect you like it does other people. He displays the pleasure and hides the consequences. That's why you can't ever believe him.

In what areas of your life has deception taken hold? Spend a moment writing a prayer to God to help you in this area.

DERISION

When he's not lying, he's usually running you down or running down someone else in your mind. Bringing up things from your past. Falsely presuming someone else's guilt. Yes, you've been forgiven in the blood of Christ, yet he keeps you scraping old wounds. Inciting doubt. He's the "accuser of our brethren" (Rev. 12:10), accusing you of not being good enough. In order for you to deflect these accusations, you need to be studying the Word, finding your identity in Christ, and praying for wisdom and discernment. That's how you refute his trumped-up charges.

Spend some moments praying preemptively for the derision and mockery that Satan may be trying to do in your life.

DIVISION

One hallmark of the gospel is the loving unity it brings to people of all nations, all backgrounds, all ages, and demographics. All in Christ. One in Christ. But Satan knows "if a house is divided against itself, that house will not be able to stand" (Mark 3:25). Anger and argument among God's people may not destroy the gospel, but they can destroy your testimony and effectiveness in sharing it. Disunity paints Christians and our faith as being weak and hypocritical.

We must not live foolishly "ignorant of his devices" (2 Cor. 2:11 NKJV). We should pray for God to help us stay focused on His will, for His Holy Spirit to keep us walking in truth, for false accusations to be thrown down, and for love and unity to reign in our relationships.

In what ways is Satan trying to divide you as a youth group? As a church? Pray against division and for unity in your family, youth group, and church today.

day 5

PRAYING WISDOM

You will notice that we are not spending time on the Prayer Strategy Target today. That's because next week we will be incorporating the Strategy Target into every day of devotions. For this last day of our week on praying specifically and strategically we are going to cover calling on God's wisdom in our prayer life.

"Wisdom is supreme—so get wisdom. And whatever else you get, get understanding" (Prov. 4:7 HCSB). Not many things in life come with this kind of endorsement. Whatever else you get. Whatever else you do. Yet anytime we hear this kind of heads-up, we know something important is about to be said. And when God is the One who's making the proclamation through His Word, you can be sure His advice is worth heeding.

How often do you pray for God's wisdom in your life and in your decision-making process?

What is one upcoming decision or situation in which you need to pray for wisdom? List it here. (Feel free to list more than one.)

Acquiring wisdom, He says, is of "supreme" importance. And prayer is one of the keys that unlocks it. In fact, prayer yields wisdom, and then wisdom yields better prayer. Wisdom is the ability to apply knowledge to a given situation. It gives you the ability to make the best choices with the data you have. To take what you know and make it work really well. To make your relationships with family work. To make your relationships with friends work. To make grand-slam, home-run decisions about your future.

Wisdom guides you to do the ethically right thing in the morally right way. It unlocks everything—things that used to seem like a mystery. When faced with dilemmas that once sent you swerving out of control, wisdom helps you locate the straight, sure path, so that "when you walk, your steps will not be impeded; And if you run, you will not stumble" (Prov. 4:12)

If you employ godly wisdom, you'll be able to look back on vital moments of decision and see that you were protected from rashness and folly. Wisdom will help you see things from God's eternal perspective, understand the cause and effect of a decision, and constantly learn from any situation. And God, knowing this, promises to give wisdom to those who ask Him for it. That word "ask" in James 1:5, not only carries the idea of asking, but of begging, calling out for something, craving it. God promises to give wisdom "generously"— especially to those who "seek [it] like silver and search for [it] like hidden treasure" (Prov. 2:4). We should want it, and want it badly.

He also says He'll give it "without reproach"—without insult or condescension. Without making fun of us for being so foolish up until now. He wants us to win. He wants to give us what we need for being successful in our families, in our friendships, in everything we do—"bearing fruit in every good work and increasing in the knowledge of God" (Col. 1:10). Because this gives Him glory. As much as He's glorified through our spoken praise and worship, He is glorified also through our integrity, our honesty, our diligence, our humility, our purity, and our faithfulness. He is glorified by us being good sons, daughters, neighbors, teammates, classmates, and friends.

How does knowing that God longs to give you wisdom help you in the current situation you just described?

For the LORD gives wisdom; from His mouth comes
knowledge and understanding
PROVERBS 2:6

As we close out our week, write a prayer to God using this verse and ask for wisdom to help you navigate whatever difficult circumstances or important decision you're facing.

List below three things you learned this week about prayer and how you'll apply these to your life.

*

*

*

NOTES

Use the space below to jot down any other thoughts or questions you have about prayer in general or what you've studied this past week.

PRAYER
STRATEGIES

BATTLE PLAN |GROUP SESSION 8

PRAYER STRATEGIES

Too often we are praying for short term physical needs and not long term spiritual needs. It is time to pray less for Aunt Suzy's ingrown toenail and more for the salvation of the lost and for spiritual renewal in the church. It is time to stop praying memorized phrases like "we thank You for this day" (unless we mean it) and time to start praying for specific people and nations; that God would bring the spiritually dead to life. How do we do that?

OPENING WORD

* Open this session by sharing your favorite answers to prayer that you have experienced this year.

* Do you know how people trade yearbooks at the end of each school year and write notes to one another? We are going to do something better than that. Take seven minutes and trade your Battle Plan book with other students and write prayers to God for each other on the inside covers. Pray something bold, strategic and specific. Get your books back and take a moment to read the prayers. Plan a time in the future to get back together to see how those prayers are being answered.

STUDY THE SCRIPTURE: PRAYING FOR BELIEVERS

Pray for the physical and beyond: Read 3 John 2 and Philippians 1:9-11

* According to 3 John 2, is it OK to pray for good health for people; specifically for believers? Explain.
* What did Paul pray for the believers in Philippi? How was this prayer more than just praying they be physically well?
* Are you praying these kinds of things for your fellow believers? Why or why not?

STUDY THE SCRIPTURE: PRAYING FOR NON-BELIEVERS

Pray for those whom God sends: Read Romans 10:1-4 and Matthew 9:35-38

* What was Paul's prayer for his native Jewish brethren? Are you as passionate about seeing your lost friends come to Christ? Why or why not?
* Would you say you have a compassionate heart for those who don't know Christ? Explain. Are you praying for God to send out workers into the harvest? Are you willing to be answer to your prayer?

STUDY THE SCRIPTURE: THE WORK OF THE HOLY SPIRIT.

God's Word says that the Holy Spirit...

* **Goes with, encourages, and empowers the witness: Read John 14:16 and Acts 1:8.**
  Where do believers get the power to share their faith?

* **Convicts them of sinfulness and warns of judgment: Read John 16:7-8.** Why is it
  important that a non-believer be convicted of sin?

* **Opens their eyes to the gospel and introduces Jesus: Read Matthew 16:15-17.**
  How was Peter able to recognize Jesus?

* **Enables them to trust Jesus as Lord: Read 1 Corinthians 12:3.** Why is it important
  that a person be able to sincerely proclaim Jesus as Lord?

* **Saves, washes, and renews their hearts: Read Titus 3:5.** What is the work of the Holy
  Spirit described in these verses? Why is it a vital work?

* **Enters and seals their hearts as believers: Read Ephesians 1:13-14.** What does it
  mean that the Holy Spirit is the down payment of our inheritance?

* **Encourages and empowers them in the Christian life: Read Ephesians 5:17-20.**
  What does it mean to be filled with the Holy Spirit?

Now that you see what the Holy Spirit can do and does, you can better pray for people and ask your
Heavenly Father to do one or more of these things in your life or in the lives of others depending
upon where they are in their spiritual journey.

WHAT DO I DO NOW?

* At your home, set up a specific room, closet, or place that can be your "war room" where you
  will secretly pray to God on a regular basis and record ways God answeres your prayers.

* Close by praying for one another that God continues to make each of you more like Christ
  and helps you walk intimately and faithfully with Him in the days and years ahead!

WHAT CAN I EXPECT

This week, every day of devotions will focus on a different Prayer Target. This will help you be
strategic and more focused as you become a powerful prayer warrior.

day 1

PRAY FOR YOUR FAMILY

It's time to get specific. Let's start directing our prayers to develop an intentional battle plan for people in our lives. Oftentimes, we pray that all the family is safe, that God bless all the missionaries, and that there be peace on earth. Those are wonderful prayers, but we need to get specific. We want you to develop a list of those you are going to pray for and how. Some of these categories will be easy and some of these will be challenging.

Let's begin with your family. Regardless of your current family situation, each of us have people we consider family. It is easy to resort to worrying about our family or attempting to fix all of their situations, but are we strategically praying for them?

How often and in what ways are you currently praying for family members?

When King David was nearing his death, he prayed over the entire nation of Israel but eventually he focused his prayer specifically upon his family. For the whole nation to hear, this father prayed a special prayer concerning his son. Read 1 Chronicles 29:18-19 and notice what he asked of the Lord.

18 O Lord, the God of Abraham, Isaac and Israel, our fathers, preserve this forever in the intentions of the heart of Your people, and direct their heart to You; 19 and give to my son Solomon a perfect heart to keep Your commandments, Your testimonies and Your statutes, and to do them all, and to build the temple, for which I have made provision.

1 CHRONICLES 29:18-19 (NASB)

What are some of the specific things that David prayed for Solomon?

 As David prayed targeted prayers for his son, we need to get specific concerning our prayer targets for our family. In the chart below, fill out the names of your family members and how you want to pray for each one of them. What pivotal prayers need to be offered up regarding each family member?

Do some research and find at least two or three Bible verses you can pray over each one as well. Scripture-saturated prayers (John 15:7) provide powerful clarity. You may have to do some work to find verses, but it will be worth the time. Whether you use a commentary, your Bible index, or an Internet search, find verses with which to target these prayers. In addition, select what days you want to pray for each family member. It may be every day or you may want to focus on certain family members on pivotal days.

Name	Prayer Needs	Verses to Pray	Days to Pray

As you close today, commit to praying targeted prayers for family every day this week. Each day of homework in this session will introduce a new group of people to target with your prayers. Like David, don't cease to pray for those in your care.

This week, we will have a Prayer Strategy Target each day. We'll provide specific points to pray for each person in that Day's lesson. Of course, remember some of the general prayers that could apply to anyone, but let's spend some time thinking about praying for those closest to us in this time together.

PRAY THESE THINGS FOR YOURSELF AND YOUR POTENTIAL FUTURE SPOUSE.

* Walk in integrity, keep promises, and fulfill commitments. (Psalms 15; 112:1–9)

* Be patient, kind, hard to offend, and quick to forgive. (Eph. 4:32; James 1:19)

* Not get distracted or cower into passivity, but embrace responsibility. (Neh. 6:1–14)

* Be surrounded with wise friends and avoid foolish friends. (Prov. 13:20; 1 Cor. 15:33)

* Use good judgment, pursue justice, love mercy, and walk humbly with God. (Mic. 6:8)

* Depend upon God's wisdom and strength rather than own. (Prov. 3:5–6; James 1:5)

* Make choices based upon the fear of God, not the fear of man. (Prov. 9:10; 29:25)

* Break free from any bondage, bad habit, or addiction. (John 8:31, 36; Rom. 6:1–19)

* Find identity and satisfaction in God. (Ps. 37:4; 1 John 2:15–17)

* Read the Word of God and allow it to guide decisions. (Ps.119:105; Matt. 7:24–27)

day 2

PRAY FOR THOSE CLOSE TO YOU

In addition to praying for one's family, we also need to discipline ourselves to pray for those we are around on a regular basis.

Paul set a wonderful example for us in his letters of continually praying for groups of people in his sphere of influence. Look up the following verses and note how Paul prayed for that particular group of people.

Philippians 1:3-5

Colossians 1:3

1 Thessalonians 1:2-3

Paul recognized the power of prayer and made it an essential part of his ministry. He knew the needs of those around him and prayed specifically for God to work in their lives according to their current needs.

Are you aware of specific needs of people around you? How can you be intentional this week to learn of particular prayer concerns?

Earlier this week, you heard requests from members of your study group concerning prayer needs. Have you prayed for them yet?

You have passed by classmates and teammates this week. While you might have talked with them, have you talked with God concerning them?

Read Ephesians 3:14-21 and see how the Apostle Paul prayed for the Ephesian church.

What were some of Paul's requests for the church in Ephesus?

Who in your life would benefit from a prayer like this?

Let's start getting more detailed. Choose at least one person from your youth group and one close friend to pray for today.

What are their unique prayer needs? What Bible verses should you pray over them? (Feel free to borrow from Paul's prayer for the Ephesians.) How often should you pray?

After you fill out the chart below, begin to pray for them and watch to see how God works in their lives.

Category	Name	Prayer Needs	Verses to Pray	Days to Pray
Person in Your Group				
Friend				

PRAYING FOR OTHER BELIEVERS

If you haven't already done so, write the names of some other believers in the target on page 123, then use these verses and strategies to pray for them. Additional prayer targets available for download at www.lifeway.com/BattlePlan

* That they would fully surrender their lives to the lordship of Jesus Christ. (Rom. 10:9–10; 12:1–2)

* Grow in Christ and obey the Word of God as a disciple. (John 8:31–32)

* Walk in love, kindness, and favor with the lost and believers around them. (Col. 4:5–6)

* Know the hope, riches, and power of their inheritance in Christ. (Eph. 1:18–19)

* Be devoted to prayer in secret and corporately in the church. (Matthew 6:6; 18:19–20; Col. 4:3)

* Repent of daily sins and walk in holiness before God. (2 Cor. 6:17; Eph. 5:15–18)

* Break free from any bondage, stronghold, or addiction in their lives. (John 8:31, 36; Rom. 6:1–19, 2 Cor. 10:4–5)

* Live with Christ as their hope and true source of peace and happiness. (John 4:10–14)

* Share the gospel and faithfully make disciples of others in their lives. (Matt. 28:18–20)

* Be found faithful when they stand before God. (Matt. 25:21; 1 Tim. 1:12; 2 Tim. 4:7)

day 3

PRAY FOR GOSPEL WORKERS

The Enemy is prowling around like a roaring lion seeking someone to devour (1 Pet. 5:8) and his target is often those in leadership.

Pastors and ministry leaders pray for many people, but how many people pray for them? We should be thankful for these effective prayers that are lifted up by these gospel workers on our behalf (Jas. 5:16), but we must also not neglect to pray for them in return.

The Apostle Paul viewed the Philippian church as a place full of ministers and missionaries for the gospel. In his introductory words to the church in Philippi, he prayed for these gospel workers.

Read Philippians 1:3-11 and circle or underline specific things for which Paul prayed.

³ I give thanks to my God for every remembrance of you, ⁴ always praying with joy for all of you in my every prayer, ⁵ because of your partnership in the gospel from the first day until now. ⁶ I am sure of this, that He who started a good work in you will carry it on to completion until the day of Christ Jesus. ⁷ It is right for me to think this way about all of you, because I have you in my heart, and you are all partners with me in grace, both in my imprisonment and in the defense and establishment of the gospel. ⁸ For God is my witness, how deeply I miss all of you with the affection of Christ Jesus. ⁹ And I pray this: that your love will keep on growing in knowledge and every kind of discernment, ¹⁰ so that you can approve the things that are superior and can be pure and blameless in the day of Christ, ¹¹ filled with the fruit of righteousness that comes through Jesus Christ to the glory and praise of God.

PHILIPPIANS 1:3-11

Paul did not pray for these gospel workers out of a sense of obligation. How does he describe his spirit of prayer for them (v. 4)?

We are often tempted to notice the mistakes our church leaders make and focus on what needs to be fixed. Paul prayed specifically that God would complete the good work He started in this church and also that these leaders would be pure and blameless on the day of Christ. This implies that they are not perfect yet, but Paul prayed that God would grow them in their love and knowledge to be more like Him.

Understanding that your own church leaders are not perfect, how can you pray for them according to these verses?

What else did you notice about Paul's prayers for these gospel workers?

It's time to pray for those who pray for others. While these men and women do great things for the Kingdom, they are still flesh and blood and tempted and tried like each of us. They need our prayers!

Select at least one church staff member to pray for. Also, select a missionary for whom you can pray. If you don't know one personally, ask your church staff member to give you the name of a missionary as well as their prayer needs.

Let's move past vague prayers and generic lists. In this prayer focus, we must do more than just ask simple blessings or safety over categories of ministers and missionaries. Who are these actual people? In what specific ways should you pray for them?

Fill out the chart below completely and get to work praying for these gospel workers today!

Category	Name	Prayer Needs	Verses to Pray	Days to Pray
Church Staff Member				
Missionary				

PRAYING FOR YOUR PASTOR/MISSIONARIES:

If you haven't already done so, write the name of your pastor and another minister or missionary in the target on page 123, then pray for them using the Scriptures and requests below. Additional prayer targets available for download at www.lifeway.com/BattlePlan

* That they would love the Lord with all their heart, mind, soul, and strength. (Matt. 22:36–40)

* Honor Christ in heart, words, and actions. (Ps. 19:14; 1 Cor. 11:1; 1 Tim. 1:17; Heb. 5:4)

* Abide in Christ and be devoted to prayer, relying on God. (Acts 1:14; Rom. 12:12; Col. 4:2)

* Rightly divide the Word of truth and communicate the gospel with clarity. (1 Cor. 4:2; Eph. 6:17; 1 Thess. 2:13; 2 Tim. 2:15; 4:2)

* Have a heart for the lost and be effective and fruitful in sharing the gospel. (Mark 16:15; Luke 10:2; 1 Pet. 3:15)

* Provide prayer, encouragement, and resources to undergird their work spiritually and financially. (Isa. 56:7; Phil. 4:18–19)

* Help them serve in the power of God's Spirit and not in the flesh. (John 15:4–10; Gal. 5:16–25; 1 John 2:20, 27)

* Help them represent Christ well in their words and actions. (Ps. 19:14; 1 Cor. 11:1; 1 Tim. 1:17)

* Grant them good health, rest, and refreshment from the Lord. (Exod. 33:14; Matt. 11:28; 3 John 2)

* Bless them with strong marriages and families amid the hard work of ministry. (Eph. 5:22–6:4; 1 Tim. 3:4–5)

day 4

PRAY FOR THOSE NEGLECTED

While we have gladly spent time praying for family, friends, neighbors, and gospel workers, the Bible commands us to pray for another group of people—those often neglected. It may not be the type of "neglect" that comes to your mind. These people aren't neglected by a world's standard but from a prayer standard.

Who are these people? Politicians and persecutors.

Throughout the Bible, God singles out these two groups of people and expects and commands our prayers for them.

Read the passages below and answer the questions that follow.

¹ First of all, then I urge that petitions, prayers, intercessions, and thanksgivings be made for everyone, ² for kings and all those who are in authority, so that we may lead a tranquil and quiet life in all godliness and dignity.

1 TIMOTHY 2:1-2

But I tell you, love your enemies and pray for those who persecute you…

MATTHEW 5:44

What makes it difficult to pray for politicians and those in authority?

Instead of praying for those who persecute you, how do you naturally want to respond to them?

According to 1 Timothy 2:1-2, what benefit do we receive in praying for those in authority?

Again we can look to Jesus' example on this tough subject. Jesus used some of His final breaths on the cross to pray for His own persecutors who reviled and mocked Him.

Then Jesus said, "Father, forgive them, because they do not know what they are doing." And they divided His clothes and cast lots.
LUKE 23:34

What words would you use to describe Jesus' prayer for His persecutors?

In this moment, do you think Jesus expected anything in return from them? Explain.

Jesus' prayer was selfless. His prayer was not intended to change their actions for His own gain, but simply to plead to the Father on their behalf.

While this day's prayer focus may not be the list you are most eager to begin, it is a clear biblical command. Select at least one politician or person in authority for which you can pray. It may not even be one that you respect or like. Pray that God would do a work in their lives.

Some of us have persecutors. Many of us have enemies. But all of us have people in our lives who are difficult to love. Put one of those people's names in the second box. Pray for God to draw them to Him. Pray He would soften their heart to the gospel.

While not the easiest list, it is essential we pray for politicians and persecutors. Fill the list and pray.

Category	Name	Prayer Needs	Verses to Pray	Days to Pray
Politician (1 Tim. 2:2)				
Persecutor (Matt. 5:44)				

PRAYING FOR THOSE IN AUTHORITY:

If you haven't already done so, write the names of government, work, or family authorities in the target on page 123, then use the Scriptures and strategies below to pray for them. Additional prayer targets available for download at www.lifeway.com/BattlePlan

* That they would be blessed, protected, and prosperous in their role. (3 John 2)

* Lead with honor, respect, wisdom, compassion, and godliness. (1 Tim. 2:2)

* Watch over, protect, lead, and serve those in their care. (Heb. 13:17)

* Come to the knowledge of Christ and surrender to His lordship. (1 Tim. 2:4)

* Establish rules and laws that honor God's law and strengthen families and cities. (Deut. 10:13)

* Submit to the authority and ways of God and His Word daily. (1 Pet. 2:13–17)

* Hate evil, pride, injustice, and turn away from Satan's lies and schemes. (1 Pet. 5:8)

* Become hard workers who faithfully fulfill their duties. (Prov. 6:6–11; Luke 12:42–44)

* Use good judgment, pursue justice, love mercy, and walk humbly with God. (Mic. 6:8)

* Be a godly example in their roles and responsibilities. (Josh. 24:15)

day 5

PRAY FOR THOSE IN NEED

Oftentimes, prayer lists in churches are full of those in need. It is very normal to pray for those who have medical setbacks, personal loss, and situations of grief. In these moments, the lists can grow very long and the prayer time can unfortunately grow very short.

Think of all the legitimate needs around you. Instead of letting them overwhelm you, begin to pray for them.

How should you be praying for someone who is going through a difficult time?

Read 2 Corinthians 1:8-11 and note key phrases that can aid you in your prayers just as the church in Corinth prayed for Paul in his afflictions.

8 For we don't want you to be unaware, brothers, of our affliction that took place in Asia: we were completely overwhelmed—beyond our strength—so that we even despaired of life. 9 Indeed, we personally had a death sentence within ourselves, so that we would not trust in ourselves but in God who raises the dead. 10 He has delivered us from such a terrible death, and He will deliver us. We have put our hope in Him that He will deliver us again 11 while you join in helping us by your prayers. Then many will give thanks on our behalf for the gift that came to us through the prayers of many.

2 CORINTHIANS 1:6-11

What about those who have the greatest need of all—a spiritual one? How should we pray for someone who doesn't know Jesus?

Read Ephesians 1:17-19 and underline key words in Paul's prayer.

¹⁷ I pray that the God of our Lord Jesus Christ, the glorious Father, would give you a spirit of wisdom and revelation in the knowledge of Him. ¹⁸ I pray that the perception of your mind may be enlightened so you may know what is the hope of His calling, what are the glorious riches of His inheritance among the saints, ¹⁹ and what is the immeasurable greatness of His power to us who believe, according to the working of His vast strength.

EPHESIANS 1:17-19

With needs so great, we cannot rely on our own power to remedy such situations. We must rely on the power of God. As we plead with Him in prayer, we expect great things from Him because we know that He is able to do even more than what we could ask from Him (Eph. 3:20).

Select at least one person for each of the categories below. Get specific in the prayer needs, verses to pray, and how often to pray. In addition to praying for these people, make contact with them and let them know that you prayed for them.

For the person in need, a simple message telling him or her that you prayed and a verse you prayed would serve as a huge encouragement. For the person who doesn't know Jesus, a simple message saying that you had him or her on your mind and wanted to know if there was something for which you could pray could open up some doors to the gospel.

Category	Name	Prayer Needs	Verses to Pray	Days to Pray
Person in Need				
Lost Person				

PRAYING FOR THE LOST:

If you haven't already done so, write the names of lost family or friends in the target to the right and then use the Scriptures and strategies below to pray specifically for them. Additional prayer targets available for download at www.lifeway.com/BattlePlan

* That God would connect them to genuine believers and the simplicity of the gospel. (Rom. 1:16; 1 Tim. 2:5–6)

* Disconnect them from influences that are pulling them away from Christ. (John 7:47–52)

* Expose the lies they've believed that have kept them from Christ. (2 Cor. 4:4)

* Show mercy, bind Satan, and turn them from darkness to light so they may receive forgiveness of sins. (Luke 19:10; Acts 26:18)

* Convict them of sin, God's coming judgment, and their need for a Savior. (John 3:18; 16:8–9; 1 Cor. 1:18; Eph. 2:1)

* Save them, change their hearts, and fill them with God's Spirit. (Ezek. 36:26; John 3:16; Eph. 5:18)

* Help them be baptized and get plugged into a Bible-teaching church. (Matt. 28:18–20)

* Help them live with Christ as their hope and true source of peace and happiness. (John 4:10–14)

* Deliver them from evil, the devil's traps and schemes, and any strongholds. (2 Cor. 10:4–5)

* Help them abide in Christ and live according to His will. (John 15:1–17)

We hope that the strategy for prayer that you have been building over these last eight weeks will guide your prayer life for the future.

May the Lord bless you and keep you as you follow after Him in all the areas of your life.

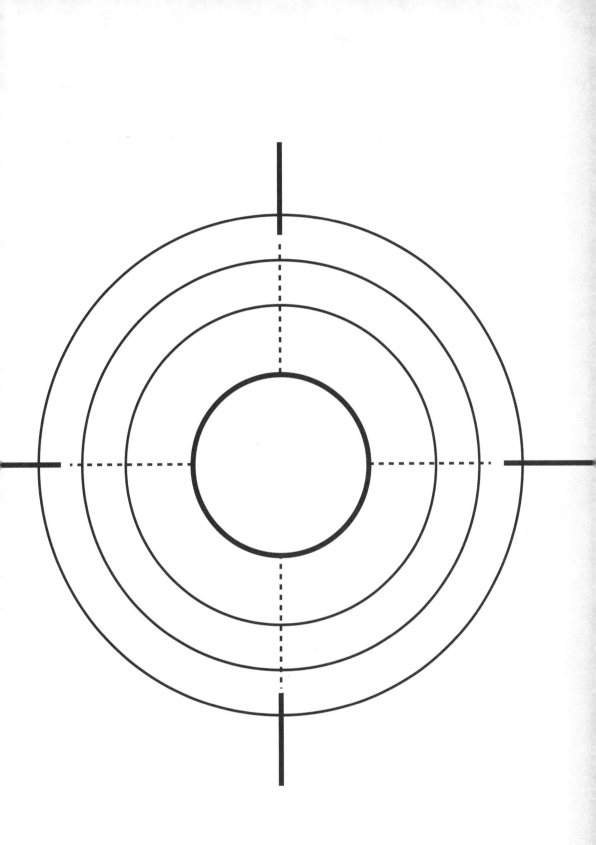

LEADER TIPS

SESSION 1

Begin by welcoming the group and distributing the student books. Share a brief testimony about your own prayer life and what your goals for this study are. Lead group in prayer.

OPENING WORD

Lead students through the activity. Be prepared to talk about an awkward moment of prayer you have experienced.

STUDY THE SCRIPTURE

Make sure all students have access to a Bible. Be prepared to lead the discussion on each passage.

WHAT DO I DO NOW?

Consider allowing students to complete their sentences on a personal sheet of paper or a poster board.

WHAT CAN I EXPECT?

Point out the five devotions they are to complete before the next session. Discuss how important it is that they complete these devotions. Encourage them to fill out the Weekly Summary page, jotting down any thoughts or questions they might have about the study.

SESSION 2

Begin by reviewing what was studied in the Group Session and what they discovered in their devotions during the week.

OPENING WORD

Lead students through the activity. Be prepared to discuss your calendar and how you use your time.

STUDY THE SCRIPTURE

Be prepared to lead the discussion on each passage. Make sure students understand what we mean by "spontaneous prayer." Be prepared to share a brief testimony on how spontaneous prayer works in your life.

WHAT DO I DO NOW?

Lead students to set the time and place they will use as their prayer time.

WHAT CAN I EXPECT?

Point out the five devotions they are to complete before the next session. Discuss how important it is that they complete these devotions. Encourage them to fill out the Weekly Summary page, jotting down any thoughts or questions they might have about the study.

SESSION 3

Begin by reviewing what was studied in the Group Session and what they discovered in their devotions during the week.

OPENING WORD

Lead students through the activity. Consider writing their responses on a white board or large sheet of paper.

STUDY THE SCRIPTURE

Be prepared to lead the discussion on types of prayers. Discuss the importance of each element.

WHAT DO I DO NOW?

Lead students during the prayer time, using ACTS as your guide. Consider allowing students to write some of their prayers on personal sheet of paper or on the board or large sheet.

WHAT CAN I EXPECT?

Point out the five devotions they are to complete before the next session. Discuss how important it is that they complete these devotions. Encourage them to fill out the Weekly Summary page, jotting down any thoughts or questions they might have about the study.

SESSION 4

Begin by reviewing what was studied in the Group Session and what they discovered in their devotions during the week.

OPENING WORD

Lead students through the discussion.

STUDY THE SCRIPTURE

Consider allowing students to work in small groups to tackle both the locks to prayer and the keys to prayer. Be prepared to share how you have experienced locks and keys in your prayer life.

WHAT DO I DO NOW?

Lead students through the assessment. Share your assessment and allow students to also share theirs.

WHAT CAN I EXPECT?

Point out the five devotions they are to complete before the next session. Discuss how important it is that they complete these devotions. Encourage them to fill out the Weekly Summary page, jotting down any thoughts or questions they might have about the study.

SESSION 5

Begin by reviewing what was studied in the Group Session and what they discovered in their devotions during the week.

OPENING WORD

Set up obstacles for the activity. Enlist spotters to keep people safe during the activity. Be prepared to share a testimony about a time when you listened to the wrong voice.

STUDY THE SCRIPTURE

* Consider splitting the group in half, with one group reading and discussing Scripture on schemes, and the other discussing Scripture on the Christian's response.
* Be prepared to share a brief testimony on how you have fallen to the schemes and how you have responded correctly. Allow students to share similar stories.

WHAT DO I DO NOW?

Lead students through the assessment.

WHAT CAN I EXPECT?

Point out the five devotions they are to complete before the next session. Discuss how important it is that they complete these devotions. Encourage them to fill out the last page of the devotions section, jotting down any thoughts or questions they might have about the study.

SESSION 6

Begin by reviewing what was studied in the Group Session and what they discovered in their devotions during the week.

OPENING WORD

Lead the discussion of the questions. Share briefly on what it means to pray in faith.

STUDY THE SCRIPTURE

* List the four aspects of what it means to pray in faith (confidence, believing, without doubting, boldly) on separate large sheets of paper. Allow students to read the Scripture for each aspect, then write on the paper what each one means, according to the passage.
* Lead the discussion through each passage.

WHAT DO I DO NOW?

Lead students through the prayer that combines these aspects.

WHAT CAN I EXPECT?

Point out the five devotions they are to complete before the next session. Discuss how important it is that they complete these devotions. Encourage them to fill out the last page of the devotions section, jotting down any thoughts or questions they might have about the study.